A runner-up in
the Thomas Cook Travel Book Awards, 1980.

With no precise route
mapped out, with no timetable to keep to, James Barclay
wandered for months through central Borneo. He
travelled up mountains and down rivers and lived with
fascinating people — Ibans, Kenyahs, Kayans, Kelabits
and the nomadic Penans. And then he
went back for more.

This is his account, always engaging, often hilarious, at
times exciting, of his adventures in one of the world's
most surprising wildernesses.

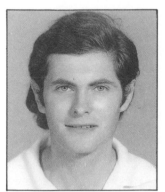

James Barclay was born in
London and continues to use it
as his base. Since leaving
school in 1970 he has spent
most of his time either working
or travelling abroad. Recently
he wrote a book, Travelling
Hopefully, about the South
Pacific. At present he is
planning a trip to the gold-rush areas of
South America.

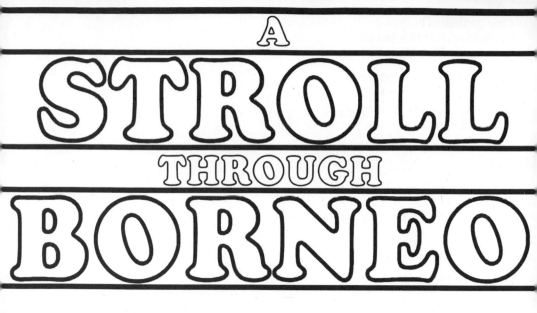

A STROLL THROUGH BORNEO

by
JAMES BARCLAY

Additional photography
by DENNIS LAU

JANUARY BOOKS

First published in 1980
by Hodder and Stoughton Ltd,
Sevenoaks, Kent, U.K.

This revised edition published
in 1988 by January Books Ltd,
35 Myrtle Crescent, Wellington,
New Zealand.

Additional photographs
© Dennis Lau 1988, on the cover
and on pages 8, 20, 24, 32, 34, 38, 41,
56, 71, 82, 105, 114, 118, 135, 141, 143,
152, 156, 170, 178 and 205.

Design by Chua Ban Har.

ISBN 0-9597806-3-7.

Correspondence should be sent to
Design Business (S) Pte Ltd
Block 809 French Road, #06-160
Kitchener Complex, Singapore 0820.

Production supervision by
Design Business (S) Pte Ltd
Block 809 French Road, #06-160
Kitchener Complex, Singapore 0820.

Printed by
Rayon Printers Pte Ltd
1002 Aljunied Avenue 5, #04-07
Singapore 1438.

Cover: A Penan of the upper
Baram valley — Photograph by
Dennis Lau.

Introduction

$\mathcal{J}$ames Barclay came into my office in Borneo and asked if I would like a story about Libya. That was easy. 'Too far away,' I said. 'I want stories about Borneo.'

'I'll see what I can do,' he said.

I was editor of the weekly Borneo Bulletin, published in Brunei and circulating in Sabah and Sarawak as well. Barclay, newly arrived from Libya where he worked with seismic survey teams looking for oil, was doing similar work in Sarawak. He seemed unfazed by the switch from desert to jungle.

Some months later, he called again. 'I've just been up the Balui river,' he said. He described some of his experiences and asked if I would be interested in a written account. 'Yes,' I said.

And that is how I helped launch James Barclay as a writer. His stories made good reading and led, months later in London, to his selling the idea of this book. The first edition of *A Stroll Through Borneo* appeared in 1980. A few years, and a few strolls, later I was able to take over as publisher, and this revised and extended edition is the result.

As editor of the Borneo Bulletin, I had frequent dealings with Dennis Lau, a talented Sarawak photographer whose pictures we published each week as one of the paper's most popular features. Now a selection of them enlivens these pages as well.

Lau recently published a book of photographs of Borneo's Penans, one of the few remaining tribes of nomadic hunters and gatherers left anywhere in the world. Barclay also spent much time with the Penans, living much as they did and noting cultural aspects I have not seen recorded elsewhere. His passages about these people I find among the most engaging in this interesting and entertaining book.

Wherever he went, up mountains and down rivers, Barclay met with adventures and experiences worth relating, especially as he has a style which perfectly matches his material. He joined in the lives and journeys of the people he met, at times with hilarious results. And he viewed the inevitable changes going on virtually everywhere he went with compassion and understanding.

In a foreword to the first edition of this book, Malcolm MacDonald, a former British commissioner general in southeast Asia, said that Barclay's book displays 'profound understanding, great wisdom and heartfelt affection for the indigenous people of Borneo'.

Hugh Mabbett
Wellington, New Zealand.
May, 1988.

Sarawak no longer numbers its administrative divisions. Each one is now named after its main town. Thus the First Division is now the Kuching Division, the Third is named after Sibu, the Fourth after Miri, and so on.

Contents

1

A Longhouse Party

I came to Borneo to work for a firm of seismic contractors who were surveying jungle areas for an oil company. In keeping with the ideas of many English people, I thought I was coming to a land of wild men and headhunters; instead I quickly found that people were friendly and hospitable. Soon after my introduction to the country I was invited to a festival, a Gawai, to celebrate the beginning of the rice planting season.

I arrived at a great Iban longhouse at least two hundred and fifty yards long and filled with families. It was about six o'clock in the evening, just as the day was drawing to a close and in a mere half hour it would be dark. My friend hurriedly showed me where to put my things, which was on the platform between the roof and the main floor where the unmarried men slept.

Then down to the river to wash. It was slender, meandering and some distance from the longhouse; and so narrow that the trees growing along the banks met overhead. Groups of girls clad in sarongs stood in the water, their long shining black hair hanging loose. Some were washing, others talking, scrubbing children or just idling; many pretended to be horrified at suddenly seeing a white man; they screamed and swam away from the bank. Others, more bold, laughed and tried to splash me.

When my friend and I had located a vacant patch, as far upstream as possible, we performed our ablutions and returned to the longhouse where majordomos and people of priestly status were tying woven blankets and other paraphernalia around the central columns of the communal room which ran the entire length of the longhouse. All the way

'The girls were carrying bottles of tuak, filling up anybody's empty glass and urging people to drink, drink, drink.'

9

down preparations were being made against the constant background noises of cocks crowing, pigs grunting, men shouting, dogs suddenly snarling at others intruding on their territory and being hastily broken up with oaths and kicks.

The boys in the band were setting up gongs and drums and preparing dancing areas. The house was so attenuated that there was room for several bands and dance areas along its length.

The women in the meantime were preparing the food for the evening meal while additional rice was packed in banana leaves for quick sustenance during the festivities.

We felt hungry so started to nibble some rice and pork, liberally washed down with rice wine. There are two grades of rice wine, the ordinary fermented tuak, and arak which is a distillation of the rice mash. Tuak is milky in colour and a reasonable long drink; arak is clear and lethal.

Thus fortified we ambled on to the long, dark common room, lit by flickering oil lamps. A subdued rhythm from one of the gong batteries floated down the long tunnel, and then its echo was taken up by another group warming up nearby. Girls were running up and down excitedly carrying messages, or going to borrow some vital aid to enhance their attire. Old men wandered around, benevolently smiling, looking forward once again to boasting of their past exploits. The women continued to busy themselves in domestic chores. All was noise, bustle and excitement. At least three hundred people, in close proximity, were completing preparations for a three-day beano during which nobody was supposed to sleep for more than a couple of hours at a time.

How satisfactory for a party to grow on your doorstep with bedding available against the effects of excessive merrymaking. Why should a party end if a couple of hours' sleep will ensure survival? Some day an enterprising hostess in England will provide rows of camp-beds in addition to gilt chairs.

Gradually the tempo increased. Drummers got set in their rhythm. It was monotonous and stimulating at the same time to have the drums and gongs pounding out an unchanging pattern. By the end, when the racket finally stopped and the noise continued to fill the mind, it was like trying to stop an unleashed metronome.

Tuak flowed. It was the responsibility of the girls to see that nobody was sober. Ibans love drunkenness and the high jinks that go with it, and it is a credit to the system that it is almost unknown for people to turn sour or aggressive or take offence while the booze flows.

The girls were now emerging from every door, dressed up and looking delectable. Even the plainer ones, being on home ground, were boisterous and laughing. In each hand the girls were carrying bottles of tuak, filling up anybody's empty glass and urging people to drink, drink, drink. I have never been so chastised as by these girls, telling me to 'minum', or again, 'Drink-lah'.

Soon the bands were really hot, the musicians joined together and it was time for the first young man to do a dance. Everybody dances individually, which ensures that everyone takes part and also provides amusement for the crowd. The girls watch carefully, for they like to see a self-confident young buck with rippling muscles who acquits himself well and gets rapturous applause from the crowd. Several males started the ball rolling. Their dancing was rather uncontrolled and manic, like a kung-fu fighter limbering up, but certain gestures are noted with a critical eye and it undoubtedly requires fitness and suppleness. Whatever it lacks in form and pattern it makes up for in enthusiasm and novelty. An Iban dancer would be quite at home in a London discotheque.

At each orchestra pit similar scenes of dancing were going on while the crowd drank and cheered. A hero of the dance floor would retire with a heaving chest, dripping with sweat and looking proudly about. Then in his moment of triumph he would brush through the crowd to the girl of his dreams and guide her down the notched log steps to the moonlit river bank. In the meantime a new man would be kicking, punching and twirling in the air. As the evening wore on young men who had been observed as not volunteering to dance would be manhandled by the ever watchful girls on to the dance floor. From a physical point of view, trying to resist girls who for ten years have pounded padi and drawn water is out of the question. Their strength is that of a gymnast, and they are slim, wiry and self-confident.

Sustenance for the physical effort was provided by rice in the banana leaves and also from plates containing chunks of pig fat. Ugh! Stuffed with calories, it no doubt helps to keep them going.

An important part of the festival had taken place on the day of preparation. Large quantities of rice and tasty morsels had been prepared for the spirits. They had to be fed first, and to this end innumerable bamboo poles had been erected on the paths around the longhouse. The tops of poles were splayed out to hold the assorted victuals. There must have been more than a hundred poles (I lost count at sixty) and the quantity of food was considerable.

Now, during the festival, the older men and some novice trainees were attending further to the business of spirit appeasement. The most obvious example of this was a short column of men walking up and down the longhouse (revellers never bumped into them) beating a pole on the ground every third step. One, two, clonk; one, two, clonk; very slowly they walked and walked and walked for two days and three nights. (They must have had replacements but it always looked like the same people.)

They wore long cloaks and headgear resembling turbans. Whenever they came to a post surrounded with mats they made a circuit and continued on their way. Occasionally they would chant a low dirge.

Chickens played a prominent role, but my powers of observation were getting clouded with the hooch. The most popular chicken ceremony was to take one white hen, remove a single feather, wave the bird over a plate of food, cut a slice of skin off its comb and send it on its way. Some birds had their throats and not their combs sliced.

In one or two selected places down the communal room rotan baskets containing skulls were hanging; they looked a bit dusty and I imagined they had been taken out of the attic for the occasion. It was under one of these chandeliers that my legs finally gave way. This was the moment the girls had been waiting for; with my resistance all but gone through semi-voluntary drinking I was now pinned on the mat by a wild bunch of Amazons, my shirt was torn off, a bottle was thrust in my mouth (my trousers stayed on), my head was held back and I was administered more drink. Fortunately I had conformed during the binge so a more unpleasant fate did not await me. When they decided that more tuak had been consumed than spilt I was hauled on to the dance floor to be screamed at with laughter. Dawn was approaching and out of the corner of my eye I saw the maestros despatching a trussed piglet lying on the ground — keep on your feet, lad, I tried to tell myself as I staggered off stage and nearly off the balcony.

'I need a pee,' I tried to rationalise to the braying mob. 'I won't be long.'

'Do it here,' they hooted back, and I very nearly did, but I made it to the notched log and, after falling the last six feet, crawled into bushes to sleep or die with the leeches and beetles.

I slowly came round after about two hours with a multitude of bites; the mosquitoes must have been drunk after their feed. Reforming my thoughts, I realised that we were only into day one, and I had cracked at the first hurdle. I was glad to see on entering the longhouse that I was not the only person who had succumbed, but while drunken bundles lay around, the steady column continued to move up and down. A few desultory taps on the gongs and drums indicated that the party was still in progress.

Most people were busy eating, and my friend, whom I had not seen since the previous evening, came up with a broad smile and showed me the room I was staying in. I tried to memorise the door, but as they are all similar it was almost impossible. I ate some rice, bananas and rambutan (a fruit) and a dish of shredded mousedeer gingered up with crushed chillies. I would have drunk tuak if it had been the only liquid available. Fortunately there was some muddy water drawn out of the river instead.

During the day activity was split. Some people sat in groups drinking and talking, musicians showed off their prowess, and pagan ceremonies were carried out in the privacy of family rooms. The spirits' food plates were untouched so they did not need refilling.

A football game was started on a field near the longhouse, but the highlight of the day was a cockfighting tournament. This is undertaken with fanatical zest by birds and men alike. A man's fighting cock is his pride and joy and it is common for wives to complain that their husbands devote too much of their time to them.

The contestants arrived, nursed in the arms of their owners, and then a second man attached a razor-sharp curved blade to the 'spur' on the cock's leg. While this was going on, bets were being placed with the long-house bookies, based mostly on previous knowledge of the birds' performance. When preparations were complete the birds were put opposite one another, bounced around a bit by their owners to ruffle their feathers and on a word from the referee the owners retired to their corners. The fights were swift and bloody. Few fights lasted more than a minute and usually one bird was killed, either through a cut that bled profusely until the bird was too weak through loss of blood to fight on, and keeled over, or through a deep slash that often would carve out a large piece of flesh, whereupon the bird collapsed; occasionally the bird was 'chicken', and ran after the first scuffle.

Down by the river children were splashing around while their mothers busied themselves; work continued for them.

In some of the rooms the young men began to strum their home-made guitars, trying to wheedle the girls of their fancy. One advantage the girls seemed to have over the boys in their longhouse was that they appeared to know what was just talk and what was for real. I later discovered that to facilitate 'shooting a line', people from other longhouses turned up at these festivals to try their chance at finding a wife. As in the carnival in Rio, at the end the headman waves his wand and announces that all peccadillos and other indiscretions are forgiven and nobody can bear grudges against others for what may have happened; a pleasant-sounding system which works.

The hard-core drinkers were still at it in relays, a thud occasionally indicating the head of an inebriate making contact with the mat. As the day wore on the tuak began to have a beneficial effect; but it was a thin veneer that threatened to crack at every additional mouthful. Darkness soon came upon us with a fresh round of the antics from the previous night. Everybody was well into his stride; most of the girls were fairly well fuelled at this stage, and while they did not dance individually they had started to copy the western system of dancing, and so all along the common room, swaying in the lamplight, were hundreds of moving bodies.

At this stage it was the girls who took the initiative and asked the boys whom they liked to dance with them.

In moments of fleeting sobriety it made a memorable occasion. The great longhouse, surrounded by jungle, with the small river winding among the trees in front, the occasional glimpse of the moon through the rolling clouds, the continual reverberating throb of the drums and gongs, the excited shrieks, screams and shouts of the people, the hot, sultry weather and the pleasant muzziness induced by the hooch.

Throughout it all the priests and their assistants kept the spirits happy. By the time I was ready to walk back it was the afternoon of the next day.

Ibans love these festivals and it seemed that little excuse was needed for one to take place. An untoward dream of anybody in the long-house is sufficient reason. More definite dates are created by the agricultural calendar — the beginning of harvest, the end of harvest and so on.

I found this visit to an Iban festival extremely interesting and enjoyable so I decided to make an extended trip right across the whole island of Borneo, from Sarawak on the west coast upriver into the central highland area and then downriver to the eastern coast in Kalimantan, staying in the longhouses of the local people all the way. Looking at the map I worked out that the best route appeared to be up the Rajang and Balui rivers to Long Busang and then through the upland forests until I came to the village of Long Nawang in Kalimantan. Then it looked as if I would be able to descend on the Kayan or Bahau rivers right to Tarakan on the east coast. A journey of many hundreds of miles should take me about six months.

But would the various authorities let me cross the border athwart the island between the Malaysian and Indonesian areas of Borneo at an un-manned outpost? I had heard that both countries were sticklers for visas, stamps, special passes, passport checks and the like. Neither side was keen for white people to wander around their primeval jungle. Still, maybe I would be able to manage because I would be alone.

I was particularly anxious to reach some of the more remote regions of the outback where there was no missionary influence, where local customs were still strong and where constant depopulation of old villages as the people moved to the coast meant that wildlife had become abundant. I might even catch a fleeting glimpse of the rare rhinoceros, an orang-utan or even a clouded leopard. Once into primary jungle, I hope to meet up with the Penans, the hunter-gatherers of the remote hinterland who slipped through the forest with speed and agility to hunt with their blowpipes.

I had no precise intentions, no deadlines and nobody to meet; my route would depend entirely on whom I encountered on the way and the availability of guides prepared to travel in a general easterly direction. I hoped that by going on my own and not being in a hurry, events, sights and points of interest would declare themselves without the need to probe and ask questions.

I was working in Brunei so I would have to get an extended visa for Malaysian Sarawak, and another for Indonesian Kalimantan. Next I must get up the Rajang river to a town where traders foregathered. There I hoped to pick up a boat or a canoe and so travel inland. Friends said all this sounded possible but information was scarce since few travellers of late seemed to have bothered with the interior.

'But what exactly do you want to do in the jungle for six months?' asked the Malaysian head of immigration at Miri in Sarawak incredulously, as I attempted to get him to plunge the tantalising little stamp beside his hand on to my passport so that I could be away unfettered by 'check in' dates. I had decided against an airy-fairy description of anthropological interest and study in favour of the simple explanation of an extended holiday. My gamble was looking thin when he asked me to show him on the map where I intended to go.

After a quarter of an hour had been spent locating a map of Borneo, I pointed in a vague easterly direction with a sweep of my hand. I was careful, however, to stop near the border area.

'And where do you go then?' he enquired without a shadow of humour.

'Over here,' I replied waving my hand casually over towards Indonesian Kalimantan.

'No chance, no, no, no, no. Nobody goes across the border from this side to that. It is a military gazetted area. Nobody is allowed to wander around. Belaga is as far as you can go. It's for your own good, your own safety, you know. We are trying to help you.'

'Okay. Fine. I'll go inland as far as you say, see the local Resident and work out a new programme from there.'

'Phew!' he sighed with relief, for I had suggested passing the buck and he was only too ready to agree. The stamp came up, he puffed hot air on it and banged it down on my passport. He smiled cheerily with his eyeballs disappearing into slits and handed me back my passport.

When I looked at it later I was glad to find that he had allowed me to stay in Sarawak for three months, not the one month I had expected.

By a mixture of bus, plane and boat, I made my way from Miri to Sibu on the Rajang river. I then embarked on one of the 'express' boats which plough along against the current powered by huge inboard diesel engines at about thirty miles an hour. We had to stop every ten or fifteen minutes

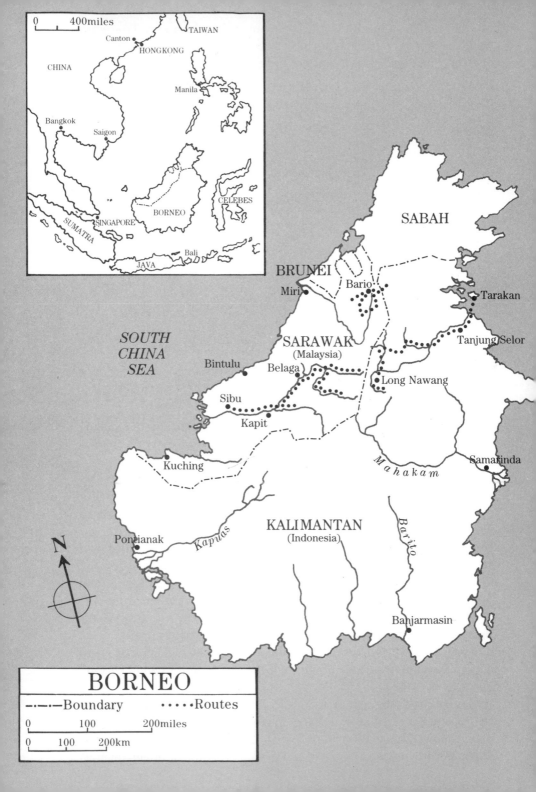

to pick up a man or woman flapping a cloth on the bank; otherwise progress would have been quite rapid. The more comfortable expresses have rows of seats, the less exotic have a banquette down each side; either way they fill up rapidly before departure time with hordes of 'shoppers', traders and people returning to their longhouses. By the time I had staggered to the wharf carrying about a hundred and thirty pounds of luggage, there was room only on the roof.

The usual rows of vendors were squatting near the wharf selling fruit such as durian, pineapple, rambutan, lychees and nuts, mostly coco or pea. The water was oily and filthy with floating debris; unfortunately the people have not changed their disposal habits with the introduction of imperishable tins and plastics. Children were running around shouting and defecating in the gutters while bandy-legged men went jogging along under heavy loads, hawking and spitting at random.

Presently the boat was surging up the river and, despite the equatorial heat, I was shrivelled up on the roof against the wind caused by the boat's speed. My throbbing head was gradually easing, but when the clouds cleared and the unrelenting sun started its scorching work it started throbbing again.

At Kanowit, after about two hours of travel, a noisy contingent of troops clambered up on to the roof beside me, dropping down their guns and knocking their sights into interesting angles. On and on we went, zigzagging up the river as a distant object waved frantically and the boat altered course to pick the person up, or to drop someone off. Sometimes, the bank would be firm and a delicate little hop had the disembarking passengers safe and dry on firm ground. On other occasions we ploughed into a thick slimy bank where passengers had to wade through mud up to the thighs before gaining a notched log leading up to the longhouse.

A longhouse is a long house, similar to a row of terraced houses, made of roughly hewn wood planks, with a roof of wooden shingles, or atap (thatch), or in the richer ones, plastic corrugated sheets. The dwelling level is raised about ten feet off the ground to allow for flooding and to enable the animals to gobble up rubbish that slips between the floorboards.

Surrounding a longhouse are always coconut palms and fruit trees, while on the river front various dugouts are tied to paddles stuck in the mud or to the raft of logs that some longhouses build as landing stages. The children, when not looking after children younger than themselves, are screaming and plunging in and out of the water. Women stand waist deep in the muddy water washing out clothes. This time-consuming occupation becomes less and less necessary the further inland one goes and where a reproachful official is unlikely to pass and throw his hands up in horror at unclothed bodies. I witnessed one incident where an official, brought up for years in a loincloth, told a European to put a shirt on before speaking to him; no doubt he had received the same treatment at some point.

At Song the party of soldiers debarked. I asked one whether they were on exercise.

'No, we're on an operation against communists.'

'Have you found any?'

'No, but we will here,' and off he jumped, swinging his rifle with the sights at a thirty degree angle to the barrel.

To be fair I later heard that they had gunned down several on this operation.

The boat arrived at Kapit at about one o'clock. Before facing the Resident I decided to buy something to read. Kapit would never claim to be an international metropolis, but it has had strong English influences, so I was disappointed to find that my choice of reading matter lay between A Medley of Elvis Presley Songs. The Complete Magician and How To Take Advantage Of The Coming Devaluation. All these books the Chinese shopkeeper explained to me were 'very, very good'.

I declined his advice and took a nap in the Rajang Hotel instead; by the time I woke up the Resident had finished work for the day. Kapit is the focal point for all business in the Seventh Division (Sarawak is divided into seven administrative divisions), and there are big plans for its future. But when I was there it was small, centred around a small square with a few shops. Perhaps the biggest advance to be discerned was a large school a short distance from the main centre. Various telecommunication towers and other paraphernalia of city life were gradually being built, but it failed to capture the spirit of a boom town.

A flying doctor service is based in Kapit and to fill in time I strolled along to have a few words with the helicopter pilot, whose geographical knowledge of this area must be second to none, and he was informative about the most beautifully located longhouses.

Early the following morning when it was not too hot, and I was sure that the Resident was in, I smartened myself up and with a deprecating air went round to his office. In the reception I was greeted by a Chinese girl to whom I made my request for an audience.

'Solly sir, no can go in.'

'Why not?'

'Too busy, lah.'

This infuriating little word, lah, is added indiscriminately for emphasis, and after a while it can even catch on to English expressions, 'No way, lah' being a favourite; but it always annoyed me; except on one occasion when an obviously pie-eyed Iban girl was asked what was the matter with her. 'Drunk, lah,' she screeched.

'What shall I do then?'

'First you have to go to the police and get permission, then to immigration if you want to cross the border.'

Over to the police station. I faced the local sergeant. Quite friendly, ten days no problem, check with police in Belaga.

'Thanks, see you.'

'And you good luck.'

Well that was easy, but inside the immigration office there was nobody (hardly surprising considering Kapit's location). I found the officer in a coffeehouse. He was amicable and even offered to run me up to see the Resident.

'But he's busy,' I protested.

'He won't be any more.'

After a motorcycle ride back to the Resident's office we found him lounging in his chair, but he hurriedly started shuffling papers, adopting a bulldog pose as we came in.

'No, you can't cross the border.'

'Why not?' I was getting used to saying this.

'Because there isn't a border check-point.'

'Can't the officer here stamp my passport?'

'No.'

'Why not?'

'Because he's not authorised to do so?'

'Why... I mean, what do I do?'

'You can only go to Belaga. You're not allowed beyond there, but I can't prevent you from going on if you wish. I just can't give you permission.'

Interview ends with a ten-day pass to Belaga. The immigration officer came up with a helpful suggestion: 'Just go and send back your immigration slip when you arrive in Indonesia.' This seemed practical and helpful so we parted with more 'good lucks.'

Before surging up to Belaga I decided on a side trip to a longhouse on the Gaat river where I had been given an open invitation by a casual acquaintance I had met in Miri called Jawian.

Staggering down to the boat with all my baggage, I realised that I was overloaded, but as much of the weight consisted of presents and trading articles, the volume would gradually decrease as I went along.

Kapit's wharf had not been designed with shoe-clad Europeans in mind. I was faced with a round log covered in green slime.

One, two, three and over I pattered, set my bags down, checked I was on the right boat and looked at the scene. A steep sloping, muddy bank with several slippery wooden gangplanks leading down to the water's edge and the devilish green slimed logs. Suddenly amidst the bustle of natives came a long gangling European with pebble glasses. On and on he

'Express' boats like these surge along the rivers, turning them into highways.

came, off the planks, and on to the log; halfway across he stopped. Then, slowly at first but with increasing rapidity, his arms started windmilling, then his legs were galloping, desperately trying to retain balance. He looked like a demented marionette on an ice slick, first 'running' forwards and then backwards, finally disappearing with a mighty splosh into the mire.

A rowdy group of deck hands hooted with laughter, and, just suppressing the urge to cuff the one nearest to me, I looked to see if he was all right. He did not come up at once, and the first thing to come floating to the surface was his passport. A man fished this out while we waited anxiously. Eventually he surfaced clutching his glasses and his lightweight bag. He had dived to rescue his glasses, and succeeded. That quietened the mob and they rushed to haul him out. Fortunately he was travelling downstream on another boat, and I was saved from savouring the drying aroma.

My boat this time was smaller with only one diesel engine roaring away, and also I was inside. This boat had banquette seating so two lines of people contemplated one another as we surged up-river. Besides the usual system of picking people up and dropping them off, often proudly nursing a fighting cock which had brought them fame and fortune in Kapit, we were constantly being reminded of the engine's noise by the position of the toilet. This was next to the engine and a regular stream of visitors to this convenience, and their equally frequent lapses at closing the door, drove me at length back on to the roof; but I was equipped with an umbrella now, and as it either rained or scorched it was never out of service.

As we turned on to the Balleh river my spirits rose. It was like turning on to a B road from a motorway. The pace seemed to drop and the special attraction of jungle and river began to assert itself. It was a large river and muddy, but there were fewer boats.

I wanted to get off at Nanga Gaat and I had primed the driver to this effect. From Nanga Gaat I had to get a canoe up the Gaat river where Rumah Mamat was located.

Eventually, while snoozing on the roof I was given a shake and told, 'You can get off here.'

'What do you mean I can get off here?' I'm going to Nanga Gaat.'

'This is okay here.'

'But why not there?'

'This is Nanga Gaat.'

My bags were tossed on to the bank.

'Hey, mind that one!' Too late. Crash. The boat backed off and sped away up river.

Nanga Gaat was supposed to be a place. After peering up the bank I detected a shed tucked away behind some palm fronds. I clambered up a rickety ladder and found a Chinese man deep in a negotiation with some Ibans. They all swung round in silence to look at this unlikely arrival. Well, here goes. I marched forward, extended a hand and said, 'Good morning, I'm James Barclay.'

The girls giggled and the men muttered something about an orang puteh, or white man. Nobody spoke English. I had arrived in the jungle.

2

Staying with the Ibans

At that stage I was still organised. My left-hand top pocket contained an English-Iban phrasebook.

'*Aku nemu mimit jako Iban*,' I said. Blank stares followed this attempt; I must have the emphasis wrong: '*Uji saup aku.*'

Still no good; the girls were giggling hopelessly at this point, then the Chinese man did something very sensible. He asked me in English where I wanted to go.

'To Rumah Mamat,' I replied.

'Well, these people are going past. They'll drop you off.'

So presently I was squashed into a dugout with my baggage and we set off with a small outboard putting away at the back. Almost at once we turned off the main river on to the Sungai Gaat. This was a delightful stream, crystal clear, not very wide and with the jungle growing down to the banks. It was a short trip; about a mile up the Gaat I reached my destination, loaded myself with my baggage, stepped ashore into a mud pocket and nearly upset everybody else in the boat. Rearranging myself I tried again; stepping daintily on to the bank I waved goodbye and prepared to shock some more people.

I climbed up another high bank with the aid of a series of notched logs, stepped aside from two piglets being pursued by a yelping dog and presented myself on the top of the verandah. Pandemonium broke loose, with streams of questions and no Chinese to bale me out. An old crone, in the absence of the men, took charge. She was bent almost double and had a toothless mouth rimmed by vivid red, betel stained gums. It looked as though she had applied lipstick to them. She struggled up and on bandy old legs hobbled towards me, and with sparkling eyes offered a greeting in a clear strong voice. Indicating a place for me to sit down she bade a couple of young girls fetch some water to wash my muddy feet. I squatted down on a woven rotan mat, keeping my dirty feet on the floor-boards until the girls came back and poured water over them.

My initial task was to locate Jawian, my casual acquaintance from Miri. My first few words were received with titters, but as soon as I mentioned his name a general 'ah' went up and his daughter stepped forward and indicated that he was upriver, followed by the word 'ladah'.

'Up a ladder,' I ventured.

'Ow.' (This means 'Yes' in Iban, and is unconnected with sharp discomfort for which they use 'eeeyah'.)

Before I could try anything else I was propelled towards a door where two bowls of food had been hurriedly prepared. I sat cross-legged in front of them on another mat made of thin bamboo strips cunningly woven together at either end with rotan. This type of mat is very comfortable, always cool and surprisingly soft to sit on, and the shiny surface makes it easy to brush the mud off.

Food revolves around rice, which is eaten three times a day. It is rice, rice and more rice. The only variable is the *bonne bouche* that accompanies it. If a fresh fat porker has been recently gunned down in the forest it will be chunks of dark pork swimming in a watery gravy. Perhaps a sleepy snake will supplement the diet, or yams or leaves. As a treat a chicken will be killed, while all manner of jungle animals from mousedeer to flying foxes are used to provide variety, according to supply. The simplest addition to rice is fern. They pluck the young fronds from the plant, boil them up and there you have fern soup. This was my first sampling of fern soup and fortunately it slipped down very agreeably, as this was to become my standard fare.

Fairly naturally the more I ate the more accustomed I became to the subtle differences between the various types, and according to my mood I preferred a bleachnum or a tree fern or the common bracken fern.

All longhouses are fairly similar in design and only vary when it comes to length. The longest unbroken one in Sarawak is about eighty doors and more than three hundred yards long. As each door represents a family unit and these units are never less than ten to twelve feet, the overall length is fairly easy to determine.

The longhouse is set well up on the bank and constructed entirely of wood laboriously shaped with axes and sharp knives called par-angs. Every plank has been whittled away to flatness with these

Girls carry water into one of the older longhouses. Inside is more spacious and comfortable than this picture suggests. Many have piped water supplies.

sharp, strong knives. Making parangs is a skilful process and is done mostly by the hunting-gathering Penan people who live far up by the headwaters of most big rivers, in the jungle hinterland. The roofs of the longhouses are made mostly of wooden shingles.

The coastal Ibans dominate the stretches of river nearest the sea. This has given them a mixed blessing. Their advantages lie in having easy access to coastal towns where medical help and industrial supplies can be bartered without having to go through a middle-man. They can then hop on a boat and return to a rent-free, carefree happy life in the countryside. They have no taxes to pay and if they want some land for a farm they just have to arrange which piece they want and then start work on it. When they are fed up doing this they can go to work for a timber or oil contractor, earn some money, absorb and enjoy as much of the city life as they want, and then return to their welcoming family, friends and farms. It is a good life in which they can enjoy the best of both worlds, but many are not happy with it. Their leaders are luring them away from their poor but perfectly balanced communities (most have resisted the influence of missionaries) to lives dominated by wages, mortgages, fears of unemployment and 'civilisation'. The natives have their own chiefs who either liaise with government officials or are in the government themselves.

How to acquire the benefits of progress without losing the simple pleasures has become a hackneyed theme, and in most places in the world it is now too late for anything to be done, but here in Borneo it is possible. A real chance awaits a leader who sees this shining light and somehow — who knows how — brings this near perfect state about.

After I had eaten some rice, the headman's daughter with two other girls invited me down to the river to wash. It is important to get the correct stretch of bank, because the romantic, secluded little creek which at first glance would seem to offer an ideal bathing place might easily be the main latrine, so rule one is to wash where everybody else washes. Being a tributary of a large river the Gaat is exceptionally clean. The fish come swimming around to nibble at the soap flakes and at times almost seem to be nibbling one's legs. The difference between a clear rocky river, easily accessible from the bank, and the muddy waters and thick mud banks of the large rivers is enormous. Swimming and washing in the former is a real pleasure whereas the latter I find particularly unpleasant; and this difference is equally applicable to drinking the two types of water.

Just before nightfall the men came paddling downriver, and with my friend Jawian speaking a little English, I was able to communicate much more easily.

'What were you doing up a ladder?' I asked.

'I haven't been up a ladder.'

'Oh, your daughter mentioned the word ladder.'

'*Ladah* — pepper, I've been on the pepper farm.'

I had learnt my first word of Iban. With this promising start I produced a bottle of whisky I had brought. One of the men who had returned was the longhouse joker. He never stopped rattling off a few words followed by uncontrolled gusts of laughter at his own wittiness, I decided to see what a good dose of whisky would do to this. I poured out a full glass of neat whisky and offered it to him; he drank it like a glass of borak — straight back in one and held the glass out for more. Another glass went down in one, at which he decided he had had enough, wandered away hooting with laughter and

25

not bothering to preface any of it with his jokes.

The others made similarly short work of their drinks so within a couple of minutes the large bottle was drained of its last drop, but the participants looked considerably perked up by it.

Seizing upon the general good humour I produced my map and began to point out to Jawian where I wanted to go next. He had assured me previously that he would like to act as guide; but as my finger sketched long treks up rivers and over mountains I could see his enthusiasm beginning to waver. One of the sages in the long-house unpegged the communal pair of glasses off the wall and they all studied my route. 'Susah, susah,' they unanimously declared. This ambiguous-sounding word means 'difficult' mixed up with 'I don't want to do it'. It was my first encounter with it, and I took it at face value. In the months to follow I learnt to ignore it or suggest that the person saying it was too weak or frightened to proceed. Another favourite Iban ploy was to declare that at least six people would be needed because of safety in numbers, but of course each man must be paid to and from the destination, thus producing a handsome bill for a relatively short distance.

The meeting broke up with an agreement to defer the decision until the following evening. I slept in the headman's room. In long-houses relatively near the coast, they unroll a mattress instead of a rotan mat for you.

The native peoples seem to have been most astute in blending their ancient customs with missionary teachings, as I was about to find out. When one turns up unexpectedly at a longhouse the customary formula is to enquire if there is a taboo on the house and if one may enter. This particular longhouse had been under taboo for two weeks since a man had died and during this time nobody had been allowed to visit and no merrymaking had taken place (apart from my whisky which no doubt had been excused by the headman). Before dawn the following morning, they were to have a ceremony marking the end of the taboo period, which turned out to be a complicated procedure as the house was half Roman Catholic.

After waking early and shuffling on to the verandah where already a sizeable crowd of subdued-looking people were seated, I listened to a recital of Christian prayers in Iban with plenty of crossing being done. Then a chicken was produced and while everybody made the sign of the cross its head was cut off and put into a large bowl, which was to be used as a collecting piece for offering to the spirits. Glasses of tuak were poured out and everybody who was not Catholic poured a little through the floorboards for the spirits. When this was nearly completed people came forward individually and had a few hairs cut from their head by the priest, while an assistant offered a blessing and sprinkled holy water. The hair was placed in the bowl with the chicken's head. Some people who had little black patches pinned to their sleeves had these unpinned and placed in the bowl instead of having their hair cut. Others gave a few cents instead.

The altarpiece was a group of dangling rotan baskets containing skulls.

As the last offerings were made, the tuak began to flow freely and everybody made merry after their two weeks' abstinence. To enhance their ceremony I visited the manang, or witch doctor, and explained to him that I had an effigy from England that some people believed represented spirits of the English countryside. If it should please him, I would like to make a presentation. He was very interested, so I produced a garden gnome from Harrods looking rather like Father Christmas. There was a gasp of admiration from the onlookers. A bedera (a plate of food for spirits) was immediately prepared for him, and drinks flowed in his honour with everybody pouring some into a little bowl which was produced for the purpose.

His name was important to them and the best pronunciation of gnome they could get was 'nom'. Nom's stature quickly spread through the longhouse. Those with a little Christian education argued that he was one of the Apostles while the majority were content to welcome a new spirit and promote him to functioning in the witch doctor's ceremonies. His final resting place, they told me, would be standing guard over the chief's grave when he died. So one day the gnome who started so ignominiously on a shelf in Harrods will be reigning supreme over the jungle grave of an Iban chief.

Following this distraction, the men left late for their farms upriver. Dawn comes about four thirty and on normal mornings by five o'clock the women are up stoking the embers of the fire to prepare some rice or a hot drink. A few of the richer longhouses grow coffee and this is always very welcome when they have it, although coffee made with muddy water loses its flavour. Muddy water after being boiled attains a particularly repellent flavour.

In the low-lying areas the best time of the day is from about five thirty to eight o'clock in the morning and six o'clock to seven thirty in the evening. This is when there is the optimum combination of coolness and light. Usually the thump, thump, thump of padi being pummelled in large mortars on the verandah heralds the start of a new day.

Also prominent in this longhouse were two bossy middle-aged women. They had something to say about everything and everybody, and in the morning I accompanied them to one of the farms where they were collecting padi from the storage bins at the farm huts. It was located on the side of an extremely steep hill; and while one woman went off to do some weeding and collect some cucumbers, which they plant among the padi for refreshment during work, the other one prepared a couple of fish they had brought with them. Another girl who was on site when we arrived was working hard at separating the chaff from the grain. Every time she slowed down she was brusquely told to keep at it, but she did not seem to show any resentment. Older Iban women become very bossy and noisy and it is difficult to tell how much of their behaviour is good humoured and how much is not.

Their political system is an anarchist's dream and it undoubtedly works extremely well. There is no system of government apart from the headman and manang who merely settle disputes and direct festivities respectively, and no class system; these two people are elected by the whole longhouse. All the people are free to marry whom they wish, but preferably each should marry another Iban who will live and work in the longhouse. Nobody takes preference over anybody else by virtue of position or birth. This makes for the happy, carefree community that every outsider is struck by when he visits an Iban longhouse. It is interesting to note that only the Ibans and the few remaining members of the Seping tribe have this structure. The other tribes have the more familiar hierarchical system and comparable advantages attached to the various stations within it.

In the afternoon I watched two women making the traditional Iban blankets. This is a craft that is dying out fast because the younger people have not bothered to learn how to do it. It is much easier to bring up a ready-made blanket from the coast. It is a pity because these blankets are popular when offered for sale near the coast and if organised making them could become a profitable side industry.

The evening brought the news I expected. My suggested route was too far and too difficult. Moreover, what was the point of going? To celebrate the decision we consumed several buckets of tuak and went to bed. The first night I had been placed in an isolated spot on my own; this night, however, the headman's wife unrolled my mattress between her mosquito net and her daughter's. I could not communicate with the daughter, but our efforts with the phrasebook had produced plenty of joviality between us. One of the bossy women had shown through basic sign language that the paint job the girl had done on her face that evening was for my benefit; so, was there romance in the offing?

The longhouse gradually settled down and as I was contemplating the mosquito net on my right with the friendly young girl in it, I was also contemplating the one on my left containing the headman and his wife, who may not have seen my point of view at all.

However, as I lay there watching the dancing shadows from the oil lamp, listening to the motor-saw whirring of the cicadas and the occasional grunt of a pig beneath us, I was distracted by the slightest creak of the door, and in a flash a shadowy figure was across the room and under the net on my right. A lot of whispering and shooshing took place and after about half an hour the figure slipped out.

I began daring myself then to see if I could continue my Iban instruction under the net. I was prompted by the desire to see what would happen. Would there be a screech when she saw a white face looming under the net and probably getting tangled up in it? Would the other net part dramatically and a parang come hurtling through the air from an outraged father? Or would — too late; another creak of the door and a second shadowy figure wriggled in. That was it; sleep overcame me before I noted his exit.

The soft light of morning came and the girl was up before I had even woken. When I first opened my eyes there was just a bare patch of floor beside me, and she was squatting next to the fire blowing at the embers.

I left later that morning, through a customary barrage of entreaties to come back. The bossy woman was pushing me around, slapping my arm and scolding me for something, while the headman insisted I could stay for as long as I wanted and his wife announced that I was one of her sons. Perhaps it is lucky I never got under that net. I might never have been allowed to leave.

I took a boat back to Nanga Gaat on the Balleh and caught the express when it came past. This was a small express already loaded with three large carcases of rusa, the largest deer of the jungle. Several sacks of live pigs about six months old, with their snouts protruding from the sacks, were rolling around the floor trying to stand up in the sacks, only to get bowled over at every lurch of the boat.

I arrived back in Kapit by mid morning and checked back into the Rajang Hotel, preparatory to proceeding to Belaga the next day.

3

Belaga

The boat was due to leave for Belaga at seven o'clock so I asked for a call at six a.m. Unbeknown to me this task had been delegated from the dapper, efficient little Chinese receptionist to one of the cleaners. This man was skin and bone, about five feet six inches tall with a bald head and a mouth that suggested he had suffered a stroke. It was lodged open at a diagonal, and inside, shining proudly, was one gold tooth. With his mouth secure in this position, the only noise he could make was a high pitched 'ung' noise. Either through his excessive thinness or a disease, he had very little control over his joints. In trying to walk his knees would bend in quite arbitrary directions. I had spotted him when I checked in, leaning against a wall holding a dustpan and brush, trying to get his elbows to work in a rhythm that would enable him to sweep up some dirt. Anyway, as I lay in slumber, confident of an early call, I knew nothing of this change in arrangements.

At six fifty I awoke, and fortunately having my baggage all ready, hurried as quickly as I could. Stopping briefly to pay the bill I saw the cleaner bedraggled on a camp-bed behind the reception desk, snoring with his kind of 'ung' noise. He was lying there wearing only a pair of shorts, and but for the noise, looked like a corpse.

'Why didn't you call me?' I asked the receptionist.

'He was supposed to,' he replied, pointing at the camp-bed. 'I've only just arrived for work this minute.'

'Well, can you get somebody to help me with the baggage?'

'Yes, yes,' and with commendable efficiency to make up for his colleaque's failure he instantly commandeered a motorcycle (the cars and motorcycles just drive around two miles of road — all there is) and roared off with my bags.

I then sprinted to the ferry point. As I approached the departure place, the gaggle of hawkers were pressing bananas, rambutans and mangoes at me. I thrust everything aside and shouting for what it was worth that my bags were about to leave upriver without me. I slithered down the plank across the green slimed log and on to the boat just as a gnarled hand covered in tattoos (this indicates a head taken) was extended to pull up the gangplank. My baggage had been neatly installed inside.

The boat trip up to Belaga is ten hours of roaring engine that leaves the brain numbed and fuddled. Longhouses are dotted up the river bank. As far as Long Pila the people are all Iban. Between Long Pila and Belaga there are many tribes, Punan, Bukitan, Tanjung and Sekapan. Before 1863 there were many Kayans located as far as Long Pila, but when they harboured the murderers of two government officials, Charles Brooke, the 'White Rajah', led a punitive expedition against them, and drove them back to the Belaga river where the small village of Belaga is situated. I imagine that to have been a front-line Kayan longhouse at that time, faced with incessant Iban harassment, must have been fairly nerve-racking.

I was heading for the most famous rapids in Sarawak. A few little eddies herald their approach, during which time all the windows are closed on the express and baggage is distributed evenly inside. I stood near the driver to watch and marvel at the incredible depth and power of the whirlpools. Often a course was run near the outside of one, and the boat, with about sixty people on board, would be flung to the side like a cork. It was a skilful process negotiating the best route through. Jagged rocks, round which water poured in powerful torrents, had to be approached at exactly the right point and angle. Smaller boats can hug the bank most of the way, being dragged round the worst parts from the shore, but a big boat has got to go where it can, and the danger is real. Several boats swamp every year and an express of the size we were in had gone down shortly before.

After leaving at seven and motoring all day, occasionally being diverted by the rag wavers, or somebody getting off, we arrived in Belaga at quarter past five.

Belaga is the frontier town of the Seventh Division. It has a small government rest house, a district office, a police station and a school; but the main feature is Belaga bazaar, an ancient longhouse of shops built about sixty years ago with massive timber beams. It is

31

still functioning, albeit in an advanced state of decay. Along the big broad verandah, natives of every dialect gather and swop stories or trade. Here for the first time one sees split ears with heavy metal rings or other objects dangling from the extended lobes. After a lifetime of adding weights the loop of extended skin can reach halfway down the breast. Only the women continue to stretch their ear lobes to this extent. The men are content to have two or three inches of loop.

Cocks are tied outside most of the shops and keep up a barrage of crowing at one another. The landing stage and subsequent mud bank is even worse than at Kapit. After gingerly edging up the muddy planks by walking sideways I presented myself, plus pass, at the police station. This was signed and given back, and so round to the district office.

The district officer and the acting district officer were both engaged away from the office. So I was seen by the third in command. Obviously anxious not to make any mistake, he asked what I intended to do.

'Proceed upriver and cross the border,' I said as naturally as possible, and adding before he could flatly refuse, 'I have a pass to enter Long Nawang in Indonesia.'

He considered this for a while and replied that he would have to check with the Resident.

'The Resident has already divested himself of responsibility. He says it's up to you here.'

'Well, the law is that no Europeans are allowed beyond Belaga; if they go they are breaking the law. However, I shall talk to the acting district officer and see you later in the bazaar.'

Next door I inquired at the government rest house for accommodation.

'Well there's nobody staying here, but we're expecting a federal minister tomorrow and nobody can stay here tonight.'

'So where do I stay?'

'Anywhere.'

This called for a beer. Settling into one of the Chinese coffee-

This Kelabit woman had the longest earlobes in Bario — and her daughter was doing well, too. The drawing above shows one of the most popular ear weight designs.

Belaga used to look like this. But these 'shops' have been replaced by a more modern variety.

shops I was suddenly disturbed by a middle-aged German couple entering.

'We join you,' the man said, pulling up chairs for his wife and himself. 'Where are you staying?' he immediately asked.

'I've no idea at the moment. They're airing the rest house for a reception for a minister tomorrow.'

'I know. These people are mad, they make my wife and me sleep on camp-beds in the reception hall for no reason; they have rooms empty, they are mad, quite mad; these ministers come here to show off, waste money. It's even worse in Indonesia; the Indonesians are terrible, terrible people.'

He paused briefly and I asked him why he was here.

'On holiday from Jakarta, I work in Jakarta.'

His wife then ventured that everything seemed to be more expensive upriver than down.

'*Dumkopf*,' he shouted at her, 'they have to transport it here.'

His aggression was extraordinary and the conditions that produced it seemed to be totally avoidable if he had wanted. Then he changed subject. 'Have you met the Dutchman here?'

'No, I haven't,' and then I spotted the official I wanted to see, and excused myself. He had bad news.

'The acting district officer says you cannot go upriver.'

'Do you agree with this policy? It seems a strange way of opening up the interior by denying European visitors.'

This contained enough priming for him to discuss at length his opinions of government policy towards the natives. A Kayan himself, Emang was able to assess the situation extremely well; and after several drinks we were agreeing on so many points that he not only invited me to stay at his house but suggested I accompany him on a trip he was making with some Kayan traders going up the Linau river to trade with the Penans. I accepted his offer gratefully; it was a good conclusion to what had started out as a disaster.

Our subsequent evenings together talking in his house gave me considerable insight into the whole problem of development in Sarawak and through his articulate and analytical assessment I was able to appreciate and observe far more from my subsequent journey than if I had proceeded without his briefing.

I was very fortunate for Emang took a great interest in developments in the interior, unlike most educated natives who are anxious to leave their past behind. He had travelled extensively in the Seventh Division taking notes and asking detailed questions from the people he visited. Speaking the local languages and being a government officer, he was ideally positioned for this, and he must rate as one of the most knowledgeable people on native affairs in Sarawak.

The following day I watched from the balcony of Emang's house as a Royal Malaysian Air Force helicopter landed and a spruce little Chinese jumped out into pouring rain. Local dignitaries jostled to hold an umbrella over his head. In this *melee* the minister skidded on the muddy path and was caught by an inquisitive schoolboy walking behind him. Emang told me some days later that this incident had produced a formal approval for a concrete path from the football field (where the helicopters land) to the village community centre.

When the minister had had a chance to meet the local chiefs and community leaders and start his speech I strolled over to see how he was received. He stood at the end of the hall with the local leaders seated in front, and the crowd standing behind them.

He was explaining in English, 'It has *already* been decided to build a hospital and school in Belaga, this has *already* been decided.'

He paused for response. A huge bearded European figure sitting in the rows of dignitaries turned round to the crowd, glanced across the rows of blank natives faces and on coming to mine gave an enormous grin and wink. Then he turned back with a straight face in time for the minister's predictable follow-up, 'But when and where, this must be studied.'

This was the first time I had noticed the bearded European and he quite obviously was not part of the official functioning. When the speech was over, after being repeated in Malay, and the minister had waited fruitlessly for any questions to be asked, he went to shake hands with the officials. Seeing the big Dutchman standing confidently among them he went forward and shook his hand first. The district officer was visibly put out by this breach of protocol.

Later in the bazaar we ran into the 'Flying Dutchman', as he was called by Emang, who explained that he had been making sketches of longhouses. He was as entertaining as his wink had suggested at the meeting. He brimmed with stories about Indonesia, and spoke so fast it was difficult to understand everything he said.

'How long have you been up here?' I asked.

'Oh, several weeks. I'm staying with one of the policeman.'

'What about your pass?'

'I just give them a sketch and they renew it. In fact I'm stuck here, they don't want my Australian dollars, and so few of them can pay money for the pictures, I'm selling everything I've got to get down to a bank.'

Then he pointed at Emang's finger. 'That looks like the ring I sold upriver,' he said.

It was, and had been traded two or three times in the course of a few days down to Belaga. It amused the Dutchman very much, but he failed to elicit how much Emang had finally paid for it.

'I live like this sketching all over the world.' His steady income, he explained, was derived from the royalties he received from several tee-shirt designs that had become internationally popular. He crossed his legs, picked a banana off the bunch that stood on each table and munched thoughtfully on it for a while, and then continued. 'I've never been in anything like these longhouses. One of them up there, a widow with two children, she's begging to come to Holland with me.' He pulled out some native tobacco and a leaf and rolled up a local cheroot. 'I gave her a shirt and told her to stay there. I mean what would she do in Holland, with her ears down to here?'

'Did she accept your explanation?'

'No, she's around here somewhere watching me like a hawk.'

Soon after that Emang and I left the Flying Dutchman looking nervously at every native woman passing by.

Further up the bazaar we met the headman of Rumah Nyaveng, a Kayan longhouse about two hours above Belaga. His name was Tujok, and he was the man in charge of the trading beat up the Linau river. He expected to be away about six weeks carrying imported goods to the highland longhouses of the interior and exchanging them for baskets, mats and knives made by the Penans. A prominent trader, it seemed he was also a driving force behind the formation of a Belaga co-operative; a hopeful method of eliminating some of the Chinese commercial influence over the natives. He was small, compact and had the successful trader's glint in his eye.

After a long discussion it was decided that Emang and I would leave for his longhouse early the following morning. However the next morning a final beer dragged into several and the sun was at its zenith as we went shambling along the bazaar, past a group of Kejaman natives arguing with the Flying Dutchman over the price of a sketch, and into an overloaded longboat.

A decorated leopard skin from Long Mesahan in Kalimantan.

4

Visiting some Kayans

The beer session before departure from Belaga turned the two-hour boat trip to Tujok's longhouse into about three after several stops on the way for people to relieve themselves. Rumah Nyaveng is situated on the main bank of the Balui river immediately below the narrow, rocky entrance to the Menjawah rapids. It turned out to be a modern construction, with concrete paths, running water and even a flower border; perfect suburbia in the middle of the jungle. Rumah Apan, a longhouse next door, was in the process of reconstruction along the same lines.

In Tujok's suite of rooms a sign hung over the main doorway: 'Christ is the head of this household, the unseen guest, the silent listener to every conversation.' These signs are produced by the Borneo Evangelical Mission. A hundred yards away at Rumah Apan the longhouse was Roman Catholic and did not sport these signs.

Now that I was in a Kayan longhouse it was easy to see the clearcut divisions of privilege. It was very different from easy-going Iban society. Tujok, a maren or aristocrat, had several rooms for his use, and other people living in the longhouse did not just saunter in if they felt like it; they came for a particular purpose or were invited.

I think his wife had much to do with the rather chilly atmosphere as she rarely smiled. Commenting on this to Emang. I learned that she had had a nervous breakdown, and for several years never spoke, let alone smiled. It was an interesting angle on native life; nervous breakdowns just did not seem to fit.

The Rumah Apan headman, one of the most skilful sape players in Sarawak, has given performances in Singapore and Hongkong. Note the diverity of items — including a gun — behind him.

That evening a binge had been prepared at Rumah Apan and the highlight was to be the headman playing the sape, an instrument similar to a guitar. Rated as the most skilful sape player in Sarawak, he had just returned from giving performances in Singapore and Hongkong.

We began with the traditional borak drinking and then assembled in the communal area, where the headman began playing on one sape with two others accompanying him. First there was a long dance of girls and then the individual performances started. A man donned the costume which had been laid out for him. This consisted of a head-dress made from a wooden cap decorated with beads and goat hair with long hornbill feathers protruding from the top; a jerkin that fitted over the head and hung in two flaps behind and in front made from bear skin and decorated with mother of pearl; a small flap of animal skin tied round the waist and hanging over his behind; a parang strapped around the waist; and hornbill feathers tied to each hand.

The man danced skilfully and to a set pattern, a complete contrast to the wild Iban dancing. The skill of the dancer was watched with discerning eyes from the crowd. When he had finished he selected a girl, who then did an individual dance of delightful grace and symmetry. She slowly turned her undulating arms to the music with the hornbill feathers emphasising the movement of the wrists. Her body rocked gently to the music, and as she turned, almost imperceptibly, she lowered and straightened her body.

When she finished she selected another man who gave his rendition of the basic men's dance, and then he selected a girl to dance, and thus it continued alternating between men and women. Emang and I were duly selected to do our best, much to the amusement of the crowd.

After a while the official welcoming ceremony was performed. The headman sat cross-legged in front of us and had two glasses of borak poured out in front of him. Then one of the girls sat down on his left and sang a long song, the words of which she made up as she went along, saying that I had come from far away, and how pleased they were to be able to extend hospitality to me. When the song was finished the headman held the glass of borak to my mouth and poured it down in one. While I drank a long-drawn 'wooo' was chanted by the crowd. Everybody clapped and then I said a few words of thanks in return, which were translated by Emang. He then went through the same process.

After this formality the evening became more boisterous. Another long dance had boys and girls mixed up together. The leader set the pattern of the dance and everybody followed. It tended to start simply, getting more and more complicated. All the time songs were being sung. Anybody sang a verse and then everybody joined in, with the chorus. Finally the girls did another formation dance, singing a song that looked forward to a fishing trip the following day.

At last the girls finished singing and dancing and then suddenly jumped up together and ran off into the darkness screaming with laughter. Were we supposed to follow?

'No,' said Emang.

So, flashing our torches, we trailed back down the concrete path, the sounds of the jungle stilled at this late hour. We lay down on our mats and as sleep was just overcoming me I heard Emang ask the headman's son if he could show him where he could find some water; and they disappeared downstairs. He had asked this in English, and even my borak-dulled brain found this something to ponder on.

The glass of water took a very long time and I was asleep when he returned.

In the morning, when Emang was washing, I asked the headman's son quite casually which girl he had guided Emang to.

'Seeling, the one wearing blue,' he automatically replied.

It was some time before an appropriate conversation came up between Emang and myself, and I was able to ask him how the glass of water had tasted that night. He was at first embarrassed, but later laughed about it.

It is a longhouse custom to have big picnics, and as Emang and I had brought several pounds of tuba root poison (used to stun fish) with us from Belaga, it was considered a good excuse to have one the next day. About nine o'clock the armada departed. Three to four hundred people from the two longhouses, taking every available boat loaded up with tridents and nets, set off up the small river flowing into the Balui nearby. The water was very shallow and most people got out of the boats and walked. The boats were poled and

Above, a Kayan woman singing a song of welcome.

dragged up the river. These small rivers have a mystical charm. The trees growing on the banks meet at the top, letting in dappled patches of sunlight. Occasionally there is a clearing where a large tree has fallen and brought others down with it. The water is clear with fresh small pools forming where the river makes a dramatic change of course. Rocks protrude from the river bed to form catchments of debris behind them. Rounding one bend we were faced with a waterfall about fifteen feet high. The river ran through a gap of about three feet between the rocks. The problem looked insurmountable, but with a minimum of effort and much shouting the boats were manhandled through the gap.

Standing at the top of the waterfall, trying to take an action photograph, I slipped on a piece of the dreaded green slime and plunged into the pool below. I managed to hold my camera above my head so that it stayed dry; luckily the water came only up to my wrists. After I had been fished out and had selected a safer site, I discovered the film was finished.

As we made our way up the river, bands of men were left behind at different points where they would sling nets across and wait for the fish. About a mile upstream the main body of people stopped in a small clearing where the river was quite wide with a deep pool on one side flanked by a pebbly ledge leading to a sloping sand bank. It was a beautiful spot, and I imagine it had been used several times before for the starting point.

A brief meal, a drink of borak, prayers for a successful day and then the first bag of white powdered tuba root poison (made from a jungle plant) was mixed with water in the bottom of one of the boats. When it had dissolved the boat was rocked backwards and forwards so that the poison slopped over the sides into the river. Within two minutes, fish of all sizes up to eighteen inches began jumping about or swimming sluggishly to the surface. Pandemonium broke loose. Men with tridents were spearing fish and depositing them, flapping, in the bottom of the boats; women and children had small nets stretched on a bamboo frame with which they scooped the fish out of the water and placed them in rotan baskets strapped to their backs. People were plunging into the water trying to pick the fish out of the water with their hands. This was more difficult than it looked; the fish were sluggish, but still had agility in the water against a pair of hands. Great shouting and excitement would break out as a big fish rose to the surface and everybody within range would try to catch it. How the people who plunged in were never speared by the flying tridents I could never understand. It looked highly dangerous. The poison can affect the eyes so people thrashing around in the water had to keep their eyes shut if they went under.

Gradually we worked our way down the river, being joined by the groups of people staged further down who were netting the fish that had escaped the main army in front. When we had got about half-way down fires were lit and some of the enormous quantities of fish caught were barbecued. Rice, cucumbers and fruit that had been brought with us supplemented the feast.

The sun shone down with just enough protection from the shady trees. It was a striking scene, over three hundred people of all denominations grouped around about twenty fires, cooking, chattering and laughing.

In the afternoon we continued downsteam, periodically stopping to dissolve more tuba poison. It was interesting to watch the relative skills of different people. The older, less agile men relied on accuracy with their tridents. A fish would surface and those rushing with nets would suddenly find a trident streak into the fish and withdraw with it on the end just as they were about to scoop it from the water.

In a separate boat and keeping slightly to themselves were three Penans who had come downriver to trade and help take back trading articles under Tujok's guidance. They were staying in his longhouse waiting to return. They were of middle height and superbly muscled. Their agility, which I was later to see in abundance, first struck me on this outing. One of them, called Peter, could run along the edge of a dugout without losing balance and then plunge his spear with unfailing accuracy into the tiniest of fish.

Towards the end of the day, weary but satisfied groups of boats came slowly paddling back to the longhouses, loaded with scores of baskets of fish. The people looked forward to spending half the night gently smoking their afternoon catch. Later in the evening I walked among the groups of people squatting next to their fires with the fish suspended over the top like silver shingles, the glow from the burning embers illuminating their faces.

The three Penans had been billeted in the kitchen quarters of the longhouse complex, separate from the main living area. I went across to visit them, but could not find them. Somebody pointed into the jungle and after a two-minute walk I found them sitting under a hastily constructed shelter of leaves where they were stripping bark from logs to make carrying pouches. They preferred to sit in the jungle rather than in the house where it was hot and flies buzzed around.

The next day I wandered round the farm area near the longhouse.

There was a wide variety of food: pepper, bananas, tapioca, coconuts, all well tended. I heard a motor running near the long-house, and following the sound, I found an automatic rice husker. This really took a back-breaking chore out of their lives. Once the rice padi has been harvested, the long, tiring job of pounding it in large mortars with a heavy pestle about seven feet long is one of the most unpleasant tasks for the women. However this machine had an opening at either end — in with the padi at the top, chug, chug, chug and out came processed rice from the other. I still have a vivd impression of Tujok's unsmiling wife regally walking towards the machine followed by Peter the Penan bent double under a giant sack of padi and in a series of gestures getting him to process the rice and then walking slowly back again with the full sack of rice now ready for cooking. Her life was too easy; no wonder she had a nervous breakdown.

That evening a small thanksgiving festival was held for a man who had been lost in the jungle for ten days and returned safely. Apparently he had had a dream that showed him the way back, so the ceremony that followed was again a mixture of Christian prayers and thanks to Bungan, the goddess whom Christianity had replaced.

The Penans were due to return to their upriver home with Tujok and his fellow traders in about six or seven days. I did not want to hang about for so long. Instead I decided to go on a side trip of my own and meet them again in a week's time. The following morning I accompanied a boat returning to Belaga. On the way we twice dropped off young children who were staying either with their real parents or adopted parents. This system of distributing children to keep numbers fairly even in each 'door' of the longhouse is very widespread. One pretty little girl whom we left at a Kayan long-house was half Chinese and half Kenyah.

Back in Belaga the Chinese community were gripped by their New Year's Eve festivities. Fireworks and fire crackers were exploding all along the bazaar, and groups of Chinese were clicking mahjong counters excitedly, and consuming huge quantities of brandy. Suddenly a tall coconut tree caught fire at the top, close to the tinder-dry construction of the bazaar. Panic broke out. Everybody rushed to one part of the rickety structure which was swaying and creaking and on the very point of collapse. Two or three men came shrieking down the verandah wrestling with an ancient fire hydrant, pulling and pushing it in different directions. It suddenly exploded into life, sousing the crowd in watery foam before it could be trained in the direction of the blazing coconut tree.

But the pathetic little jet, squirting for all it was worth, rose in an arc of about fifteen feet while the fire blazed at a height of thirty feet.

'On to the roof, on to the roof,' some bright chap advised, so the hydrant was hauled on to the eighty-year-old roof. Three-volt battery torches were trained on to the 'fireman' crawling along, but before he could get within range, a wail followed by the cracking of rotten timbers and an impenetrable darkness marked the spot where the torches were shining.

By now scores of people had gathered and a hysterical shop-keeper was trying to get people off the collapsing structure outside his shop. Frantically pushing them back, he single-handedly arrested what could have been a major accident.

The drama ended itself, the inflammable parts of the coconut tree blazed away merrily until there was nothing more to burn, spluttered a few times and left a few bright orange coconuts shining in the darkness.

Emang appeared the following morning having run out of petrol above the longhouse and spending all night drifting downstream.

That evening we visited the nearest Kayan longhouse to Belaga. Located about ten minutes up river, it is called Rumah Aging.

Before we could get going our boatman got paralytically drunk, accused an Iban of stealing his farmlands and a fight broke out. A policeman dozing nearby was woken up and promptly arrested the Iban. Just as we were about to go, the boatman then discovered he had lost his money during the brawl so another long delay took place while we flashed torches round the mud-banks. Nothing was found, so off we went.

At the longhouse one of the old men appeared and began telling stories about the past.

He began by relating how a resistance movement against the Japanese had been organised in the area during the second world war. A Kenyah had been sent over from the Baram by a group of Europeans who had parachuted in, to ask if the Kayans in the Belaga area would support the British. A long debate took place at which a decision was not reached, so they summoned the manang to decide. He killed a pig, studied the message on its liver and declared that they should help the British resistance. It was a brave decision as Japanese reprisals to native villagers even suspected of co-operating were excessive and cruel. The message was sent back to the Baram saying they would help and subsequently an Englishman made his way over to organise the resistance.

This included wiping out the Japanese garrison in Belaga for which the old man telling the story managed to get a 'slice' of skull which he showed us proudly. He also seemed very amused at the Japanese attempts to 'colonise' the outback; many of them went upriver with farm implements to try to settle.

He continued with more racy stories about the Kayans when they were living below Belaga. 'One year they had a bad plague of monkeys damaging their farms, so they caught some of them and as a lesson to the other monkeys cut their hands off and the skin off their foreheads and sent them back into the jungle. As a revenge one of the monkeys came to the village and raped one of the girls, who reported that its penis was as hot as a chilli.' General laughter.

Most longhouses suffer at least one blight of either mosquitoes, sandflies or ordinary flies. Rumah Aging had bad mosquitoes. I was bitten all night long.

In the morning, people were spreading out wild banana leaves to dry and putting padi on top to give flavour to the cigarette paper that was then made from the dried leaves.

In the afternoon, still suffering from a borak hangover (we had been drinking sour borak, a beverage that is unique in its hideous after-effects) I waved in a small dugout, and paddled down to Belaga.

Wandering round the bazaar I met a man about to take a long boat upriver to the last collection of longhouses before the border with Indonesia — to a place called Long Busang. If conditions were perfect the boat would take three days, motoring ten hours a day. I wanted to go but was in a considerable dilemma. Emang had done a bunk upriver, just leaving me a vague message and I had no way of knowing when the Penans and Tujok were likely to leave. They had said about a week, but so much would depend on river conditions and new factors might crop up; it was impossible to plan to the nearest day.

I did not want to hang around Belaga any more than I had cared to stay a week at Tujok's place. There was so much of Borneo to explore. I decided to risk being late back. If all went well the big boat should get to Long Busang and back within a week.

5

Up the Balui

At six o'clock the next morning, I walked down to the boat, which was already full of baggage and natives who were returning upstream. Two forty gallon drums of petrol were blocking most of the middle section. Attached to the back were two forty h.p. engines, with a spare one lying inside. The driver and his assistant had a small wooden cover against the elements, while the hoi polloi, squashed and wedged between the baggage, relied on umbrellas. About fifteen people were in the boat, and at seven a.m. the engines were started and away we went.

The boat was coping quite well with the turbulent waters, but then ahead of us was a narrow channel with foaming, mountainous water, gushing and rushing through it. This was the notorious Bakun rapid.

Just below it we stopped by the bank and everybody got out to walk around the tricky patch. I asked to stay in to take some photographs.

'Okay, but you better get your boots off,' said the driver.

We then backed down a little way, revved the engines up to maximum and zoomed towards the roaring passage. Whoosh ... we were through the fastest part of the stream and heading diagonally towards a patch of calmer water. The engines were screaming at full power, and we seemed to be making no headway at all. The possibility of what would happen if we could not make the calmer patch began to dawn on me, and I turned to look at the driver. His face was a grim mask as he undoubtedly cursed my extra weight. We inched our way forwards with the noise of the engines drowned by rushing water splashing off the rocks around us. I saw for the first time the fuss that everybody makes about getting boats up these rapids. One engine needed only to falter for a few seconds and we

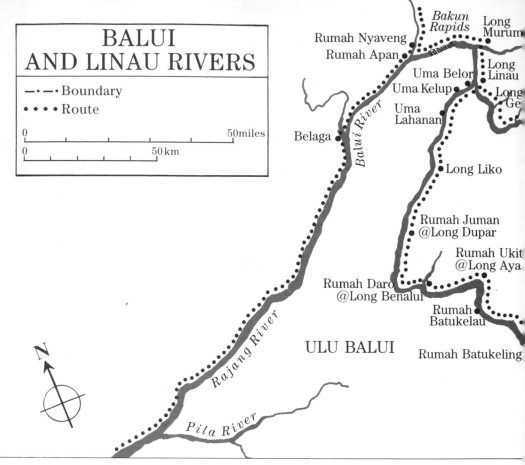

BALUI AND LINAU RIVERS

—·—· Boundary
•••• Route

0   50miles
0   50km

Bakun Rapids   Long Murum
Rumah Nyaveng
Rumah Apan
Uma Belor   Long Linau
Uma Kelup   Long Ge
Uma Lahanan
Belaga
Balui River
Long Liko
Rumah Juman @Long Dupar
Rumah Ukit @Long Aya
Rumah Daro @Long Benalui
Rumah Batukelau
Rumah Batukeling
ULU BALUI
Rajang River
N
Pila River

would be overwhelmed.

We eventually got into the calmer water, which was still flowing extremely swiftly and immediately swung the back of the boat round so that we were working our way diagonally towards the other bank. Thus we achieved the sanctuary of slower waters and picked up the other passengers, who had made their way over the cliff bordering the river.

The water after this was choppy but quite negotiable and I was able to concentrate on the delightful Kenyah girls wedged beside me. They were on their way back to Long Busang, the last village on the Balui. Many of the younger people from the big longhouses and kampongs have learned some English from the small schools recently started at their villages. Where parents can afford to be without an extra pair of hands, the children are boarded and educated in Belaga.

While I was embroiled in a pidgin English conversation with the girls over how to open a tin of curry with just a knife, the boat diver-

ted towards the bank where a large figure was standing. As we came closer I saw clearly that it was Emang.

We could not stop because the bank was rocky and the water rough, but maintaining a slow headway, the driver had a few shouted words with Emang. Then the engines opened up again just as Emang spotted me. He tried to call a message above the noise; he gesticulated and shouted. I waved back as if he was just being friendly, and returned to the problem of the curry tin with my new friends.

However I soon had my doubts. What a waste of effort it would be if I went on this trip to Long Busang only to find immediately I returned that Tujok had gone without me. If I had spoken to Emang, I could have found out whether Tujok and the Penans were due to leave soon. Of course I could always travel inland entirely on my own but the Penans would be intriguing companions and Tujok's trip was a rare opportunity to go up the Linau river where big boats could not go. I endeavoured to console myself by realising that I was not on a schedule.

As the sun was showing signs of setting, we arrived at Long Dupar, a Kayan longhouse where the penghulu, or chief, for this stretch of the Balui lived. The people in the boat, after being fried under a grilling sun, amplified by the reflection off the water, sprang out of the boat like men being released from a clay pigeon ejector. They knew the form, so I followed in their wake. A spare room in the longhouse had been set aside for us and immediately they bagged the best places, leaving the driver and me on a ledge up a narrow ladder. The girls collected wood, chopped it up and got a fire going while the men puffed on their cheroots.

The penghulu was away, so I wandered along to pay my respects to the headman. He had one eye and was a committed Christian. The B.E.M. (Borneo Evangelical Mission) had done their work well. Instead of borak drinking and dancing, there were long prayer sessions.

'We don't have any borak drinking here,' the headman proudly told me.

I thought I would test that, so I produced a Mickey Mouse watch which I dangled about saying, 'I'm so desperate for a glass of borak I'd give this watch for a bottle. It's pity you don't have any.' Sure enough, a young woman slipped away and returned a short time later with a bottle of pink borak, and claimed her watch.

I returned to the crowd, put down my bottle and went to find a glass. I was gone only two minutes, but when I returned one of them had his head tilted back with the neck of the bottle halfway down his throat and the contents draining out more quickly than emptying bath water.

'Hey, that cost me a Mickey Mouse watch!' I exclaimed as I retrieved my bottle which made an uncorking noise as it broke free from his mouth.

During the night it poured and poured. A storm, with blinding flashes of lightning lasting several seconds and illuminating the sky like daylight, deafened us with claps of thunder that shook the whole building. I thought no more about it until the morning when I took one look at the river and saw a raging torrent.

'How long will that take to go down?' I asked the driver.

'A few hours should reduce it a bit, but we can't go until tomorrow.'

'Oh well,' I thought, 'there's going to be no chance of my getting back in time to accompany the Penans,' so donning a large straw sunhat I went off to help harvest rice. A small metal blade at right angles to a piece of wood that fitted in the hand, was what one used for snipping off the ear of the padi. It was just the women and me, working in a long line, squelching through the mud. The work was not hard, but it was hot and a certain type of fly with a sting like a nail being driven into one's arm provided the unpleasant aspect. The atmosphere was excellent. The women were constantly joking and laughing and the morning passed quickly. Stumps of sugar cane were cut and we chewed this for our lunch. Then the ears of padi were trampled to remove the grain from the stem. It was a picturesque scene with the girls in their wide-brimmed straw hats, calf deep in mud against the buff-coloured stalks of padi, their extended ears and flashing smiles; the river behind carrying quantities of debris washed into it by the rain; the brilliant blue sky grazed here and there with washy streaks of white cloud. I sat in the shadow of a pepper plant and watched their carefree manner and effortless grace and charm.

Towards the late afternoon the river had gone down a bit, but still not nearly enough for us to leave, and while sitting forlornly with the others I was asked to go and see a sick man. He lay in a small recess with one leg bent up. His knee had a large septic sore on it. He needed penicillin, but I did not have any. Although quite young, he seemed to have given up. He hardly ate and was pitifully thin. I could only suggest they take him to Long Linau where there was a small clinic, but I could see that they were resigned to leaving him alone.

I returned to the verandah, and was watching a mat being woven when in the distance came the chug, chug, chug of a large boat. Soon round the bend came a splendid old River Queen, wallowing against the stream. I hurriedly paid my driver, collected my bags and descended to the bank. I waved in the ancient metal hulled boat which was thirty feet long and powered by an old Bedford diesel truck engine. It was crewed by grinning Chinese. They were making for the next longhouse up the river. All the way up, the river got progressively rougher, interlaced with small stretches of rapids. The choppy waves bounced us around and it was exactly like being at sea; my first boat would not have got through it and I guessed it would stay at Long Dupar for at least another day.

Just as it was getting dark we arrived at Rumah Daro, a twenty-door Kayan longhouse. The whole wall of the communal verandah was one huge mural depicting Kayan designs. This time I sprinted in ahead of the mob and bagged a good sleeping place.

There were many rubber trees surrounding the longhouse with their white flakey bark and delicately formed leaves of light emerald. On each stem were scars where the latex had been collected and on many of them a small silver-coloured scoop was attached to the cut, and oozing down this channel into an old bottle or tin would be the white latex. The roots around the base of the trees are often partly above the surface and it is difficult to walk quickly over them.

Although it was the harvesting season there were many people staying in the longhouse and some of them were boys making mats and baskets. The atmosphere was very friendly, and the first night an impromptu party developed. The headman sang a song of welcome, which was followed by one from the girls, borak was consumed in large quantities and before long dancing had started. It continued late and the following morning the River Queen was slow in starting. I went down to wash in the Benalui river which flows close to Rumah Daro. It was a highly convenient river with a wide foreshore of rocks, and on each curve of the meandering course a natural swimming pool had been formed. It was possible to dive in from the bank; and it was crystal clear.

By mid-morning we were getting ready to leave, and after waiting around the boat for a while and listening to the wailing of a dog from under the steps that led down the river bank, I wandered casually over to see why it was making this noise. I found it with a large gaping wound crawling with maggots; this in itself was not so extraordinary, but what I did find surprising was the complete disregard of the constant flow of adults and children up and down the steps leading over this wailing, stinking sight. They were untouched by the fact that not only was the creature obviously in severe discomfort, but that the noise was considerably distracting.

I tried pointing out the dog's plight to anybody who might have been interested, but after getting a consistently negative response, I waited until departure was imminent, then despatched the wretched animal with a spear from one of the loitering natives. As I eased the spear into its heart the noise naturally ceased but, as if in a sinister gesture of appreciation, its tail began to wag. After rounding up some young boys, I had it dumped in the middle of the river. The general reaction seemed to be one of bemusement.

With this distraction over, we clambered aboard and proceeded upriver through some more rapids, but basically it was hour after hour in the hot sun, watching the big brahminy kites wheeling overhead, the hornbills gliding across the river and the small, brilliantly coloured kingfishers perched on twigs near the bank or flying across the bows.

We stopped at Long Aya, the only Ukit longhouse in Sarawak, for lunch. It was rather run down, but fifteen pretty, unmarried girls laughing and cavorting around the place made up for any structural

'..... The whole wall of the communal verandah was one huge mural depicting Kenyah designs.'

shabbiness. Downriver they had talked about the beautiful Ukit girls, and there was certainly truth in the rumour for they were very pale skinned with delicate features. All the other Ukits lived in Indonesian Borneo. Why this one longhouse should exist so far away was difficult to explain.

A pet monkey sprang around out of control; it was black, tailless and called a wak-wak. We left a member of the crew here; the fellow who cleaned the water intake filter was Ukit and was going no further. I noticed that the older generation of Ukits were particularly addicted to the little packets of Chinese 'headache powder'. Many of the elderly natives get addicted to this potion and spend every cent they can acquire on it.

On and on we went, the old Bedford engine being continually nursed by an oil-smeared Chinese. At Batu Kelling, another Kayan longhouse of forty doors, half of the passengers disembarked, and it was now quite comfortable in the boat. I went into the longhouse and had a handful of giant bananas pressed on me. These bananas are about three times the size of ordinary ones and have the distinctive flavour of the very small kind.

Away again to Long Bulan, a sixty-five door Kenyah longhouse split in the middle by the Siva river. Here all the passengers, bar me, got off and for the two-hour trip up to Long Jawi I was on my own.

Long Jawi is a noted place in Sarawak, as it was a base for some of the British troops operating against the Indonesians during the confrontation in 1963. It is a large village of about 600 people and all the debris of fighting troops has been put to good use — ammunition boxes used as tin trunks, bailey bridge strips as floorboards. Later when I was in Kalimantan and asked people where they got their guns from, 'Long Jawi in Sarawak' was the usual answer.

There were about five longhouses here, apart from a big collection of individual huts.

We docked and I made my way up to the penghulu's quarters. He was away in Kuching, but a caretaker indicated where to sleep. It was a huge room, with a slightly raised platform at one end of the room. Covering this platform was a series of split bamboo mats woven together. The ceiling height was about fifteen feet, and above that were the sleeping quarters of the penghulu and his family. Outside on the main verandah the huge dimensions revolved around a ceiling height of about forty feet. Constructed with massive hardwoood timbers, the communal area of Kenyah longhouses are always huge. The B.E.M. had, however, made use of this natural auditorium and turned it into a church. Their services are held every evening and the most attractive part of them are the rollicking hymns translated into the Kenyah language and sung with great gusto. It is like an ancient group of pilgrims preparing to set off on their travels.

Highly populated kampongs tend to get pretty filthy and Long Jawi was no exception. Masses of debris such as rotting fruit skins (I tried to persuade them to start compost heaps, but to no avail), wood chippings, discarded baskets and pig and chicken droppings were everywhere one trod.

The Jawi river, although a tributary, is muddy and deep. I washed gingerly, and was climbing up on to the bank when I spotted a delightful girl waiting for me to finish before going in herself.

'Do you speak any English?' I asked.

'Yes,' she said.

This was a breakthrough. Most girls who speak a little English will not admit it; and if they can be coaxed into talking will do so only in the company of a band of tittering supporters.

'Well ... I wanted to learn some phrases of Kenyah. Can you teach me?'

'Yes, come to my house afterwards.'

A bunch of ragged children who had been observing proceedings went rushing around announcing what the orang puteh, or white man, was up to.

Inchan's home was one of the individual huts quite close to the landing stage; inside was the usual collection of people of all ages mixing together quite happily. A young buck with long hair was strumming a banjo in the corner. Somehow all over the world the corner banjoist has a similarity of demeanour. A uniformity in attitude seems to lend a uniformity in appearance.

She had seven brothers and sisters, one of the sisters being as easy on the eye as was Inchan. Her father, his arms decorated with tattoos, sat impassively leaning against the wall puffing on his cheroot. Most of the older men had had considerable contact with British soldiers during confrontation and retained mixed feelings about them. Her mother was much more lively; red betel nut stains flashed gaudily every time she opened her mouth or smiled. She was in the process of making one of the rotan baskets that are an indispensable item of native households; about eighteen inches high with a diameter of nine inches. They are made from strips of rotan, half of which they dye black by wrapping in leaves and boiling. Then with the skill of practice they use the black strands to pick out traditional patterns on the side of the baskets.

After my Kenyah lesson, Inchan was summoned by her mother to try and weave the basket. She had obviously done very little of it and her mother patiently tried to show her how it was done. Repeatedly she got it wrong and her mother scolded her. 'What's the good of going to school if you can't make a basket?' It turned out that she had been forbidden to go back to school until she had learned some of the useful crafts of their day-to-day life. Her mother's remark was fair comment and underlined the difficulties facing authorities and natives alike on how to go about the modernisation process.

Inchan's apparent happy acceptance at being recalled from Belaga, where her studies were going well and could have led to a regular job in a city, to go back to the jungle life of planting, harvesting and pounding padi, poling boats up the tiring stretches of shallow water, searching for jungle fruits, and generally working non-stop in the back-breaking domestic routine of the native life, intrigued me. I decided I would try to return here on my way to Kalimantan; but now I calculated that if I left on the River Queen the next morning I could, by going downstream, reach Tujok's longhouse before he set off on his trading trip with the Penans.

[I have kept in touch with Inchan over the last ten years. She is

happily married and has two children of her own. Her husband works for an oil company and they live in a small house near Miri. The last time I visited, her mother happened to be staying and was still busy making baskets with the intricate Kenyah patterns while Inchan busied herself with her children — having given up all attempts at handicraft. Some years ago she attended a secretarial course in Miri, but with the same inconclusive results as attended her attempts at basket-making.]

At seven a.m. the next morning the grinning crew started backing the boat, we swung round and with the stream with us we went hurtling downriver. We passed a group of people getting out of their dugouts to start another day on their farm. I saw Inchan and her sister, who ran down to the bank and waved as we went past. I wondered, as I watched them climbing back up the bank, hitching baskets on their backs, how they really felt as day after day they carried out the same round of chores in the grilling humid atmosphere.

We raced through all the turbulent patches, where on previous days we had wallowed and struggled. Past Long Dupar where the longboat on its way to Long Busang was still tied to the bank. The driver, with the remains of his passengers, was squatting near the bank looking forlornly at the still high river. As we passed, I gave a shout, pointed up river, and gave a thumbs-up sign. A resigned wave, rather like a window cleaner wiping the first pane of the day, was all the driver could manage.

In the early evening we reached Tujok's longhouse where he announced that, as he had prepared everything, they were leaving the following morning, a day earlier than expected. I had been saved by the gallant speed of the River Queen for I had banked on having an extra day in hand. I wandered along to the adjacent longhouse, Uma Apan, where Emang and I had spent the pleasant evening of entertainment, and asked where he was.

'Oh he's staying with a girl in a farmhouse at Uma Belor.'

He'd done it again!

As I had just spent a long lazy day in a boat, the longhouse M.C. decided that I was in suitable shape to take on the longhouse tough at Kayan wrestling. I was not going to offer any excuses, but while calling for a glass of borak to dull the nervousness creeping into my legs, I spotted a gnarled brute descending down the notched logs, with a milling group of seconds and fans.

Kenyah farmers setting out for their fields — with guns and a chainsaw.

'I can't fight him,' I protested.

'Just try, lah.'

'Quick, bring a parang, take my head now. I don't need softening up first.'

Nobody would hear of me backing down, and presently I was propped up in the ring of chanting natives, while their man did some knee bends and punched the air to loosen his arms up.

'I need another drink, I need a second, I need advice, I need a delay. Tomorrow, what about tomorrow?' I'd be gone at first light tomorrow. 'Hold out for tomorrow,' I tried to tell myself with conviction, but there was no stopping the relentless process.

The sinewy, confident fellow locked his arms around my back and I was placed in the same stance with my hands clasped behind his back. With a whoop he endeavoured to flick me into the mud, but as I had seen that my only hope was a fast start I had tried to do the same, only applying force in the opposite direction. The result was that we stayed upright wheezing and straining. The object was something like the Japanese wrestlers. The first man down, as opposed to out of the ring, was the loser.

The braying crowd were clapping and cheering as we tussled around the muddy ground. Eventually quite suddenly he released his grip, and after congratulating me on my good effort proceeded to explain some of the more rudimentary tactics of the fight. While regaining my breath I tried to make mental notes in case of any future contest, and realised that he had merely staged an exhibition bout; at any point he could have flicked me rolling over and over in the slimy mud.

When he had finished explaining I thanked him as gracefully as I could and skulked off to the other longhouse. How was I going to impress these girls if I could not do better than that. Thank goodness Inchan was not watching.

I arrived back at Rumah Nyaveng, and, locating my emergency rations of whisky at the bottom of my bag, sent myself off into oblivion.

6

Trading with the Penans

Peter, Tukang and Bujang were the three Penans who were providing escort and muscle power to our trading trip up the Linau and Kajang rivers. When I surfaced in the morning, they had already half loaded the boat with tins and tins of tee-shirts, sugar, sweets, biscuits, salt, hair oil, metal strips for forging parang blades, mirrors, batteries, tobacco and petrol. To transport all this was a twenty-foot longboat with a six h.p. engine at the back. I took one look at the engine and asked Tujok what it was for. He said it helped the paddlers a little when they got tired. The Penans were complemented by four Kayans and me. Tujok was captain; his second in command was Seego, a lean, tight-lipped man who spoke about fourteen words the whole trip. They were both traders, while the other two Kayans were crew. One was a teenager called Evan, used for carrying heavy loads and rowing hard. The other, an elderly man, Lake Livan, was in charge of the cooking arrangements and baling water out of the boat. His personal appearance was the same from the day we left to the day we got back; it consisted of a multi-coloured floral plastic stetson, an old green army shirt, and a pair of swimming trunks inside out.

He had a humorous face which he put into effect with a variety of gesticulations in an endeavour to communicate with me. He was most anxious that I should not miss photographing anything, and his sign for this was to hold his hands curled over his eyes like binoculars and point in the direction I should be looking.

Appreciating the time it took me to unpack my camera from its waterproof casing he would start his actions well in advance. Whenever he failed to convey the meaning of something to me he would scratch his head with both hands simultaneously in the manner of a monkey.

This unpromising boat-load set out to conquer a series of rapids that had I know about in advance I would not have sat so complacently in the middle of the boat. The river was at the correct level for our embarking; not too high, but enough to cover some of the more treacherous rocks.

We plunged into the first set of rapids which were just above the longhouse, and it was immediately obvious that progress was going to be slow, the tiny engine at the back doing its best to aid the pum-

Tujok, second from left, and his crew on the Linau river.

ping oarsmen. Whenever the stream became too strong, or the paddlers too tired, they jumped on to the bank trailing long rotan creepers attached to the boat and hauled it round the rocky, riotous waters. After an hour the boat was too heavy to pull with all the baggage in it, and so began the long process of unloading everything, carrying it upriver across jagged, green slimed rocks, and then pulling the boat up.

I remembered the devastating power of the Bakun rapids that the two forty h.p. engines had just managed to pull through, and I wondered as we went about our exhausting routine how we were going to manage. The approach to Bakun was a sheer wall of rock, lashed by the thundering spray from the cascading water pouring through its narrow channels. In order to pull the boat we would have to get past this wall and on to where there were some broken rocks. These would provide tenuous footholds for pulling the boat up.

We entered the boiling cauldron of water. The Penans were trying to pull us along the slippery wall with their hands. Then, just as the front of the boat was reaching the lower rocks, Tujok screamed something above the noise: the Penans leapt at the rocks; I thought this was my cue as well, but by the time I realised I was meant to stay seated it was too late. Like a fly, I was clinging to the sheer rock with my collapsing fingertips clawed into a wet slimy crack. In the seconds that the Penans leapt out with their rotan streamers, and released their pressure on the rocks, the boat immediately slipped back. This left nothing for me but foaming waters below and an im-

Peter and Bujang provided 'muscle power'.

possible climb above. Tujok was shouting inaudibly; but nothing could have altered the outcome. In attempting to climb up I plunged into the water and was swept past the boat. Crashing off the rocks and buffeted by the counter currents, I still had time to hope like hell that I would not be sucked into some underwater rocky crevice by the undertow. A hundred yards down I was ejected into calmer water and swam to the bank which, being beyond the rapid, was about thirty yards away. I made my way over the cliff back upstream, in time to see the final stages of manoeuvring the boat up. Lake Livan, clearly visible in his stetson, was concentrating on making his way over the rocks, while the Penans were engaged in the real difficulties and dangers of getting the boat through.

They sprinted over the rocks, plunged into horrific whirlpools of water and still managed to find footholds to take the strain of the boat. No normal boat crews would take these risks. They would cut a path round the bank and drag the boat. But these people were going home bearing gifts and goods, and this incentive drove them to their monumental efforts and risks.

At last the boat was round safely. The following day, two boats of the same size went down losing a total of three new forty h.p. outboard engines plus assorted baggage. The excitement engendered, the split-second timing required in bringing a small boat up safely, is totally lost in the big River Queens, and it means of course that fewer and fewer people learn the skills and intuitions of comprehensive riverine travel.

The whole of the day we spent in struggling up this section of uncertain water. It ends a short way below Long Murum. Above Long Murum the water is more peaceful until one turns into the Linau river. Almost immediately, if the water is fairly low, there is a tricky channel to negotiate. Time and time again it was only the unbelievable agility of Peter, Bujang and Tukang in finding footholds among submerged rocks that got us through. Often they were totally submerged with the rotan creepers mysteriously being drawn forward by a sub-aqua winch. One would sprint along the slippery rocks, take the strain on the creeper, while the others caught him up and hauled the boat forwards. Tujok would be manning the pathetic little engine and shouting directions.

We checked into a farmhouse belonging to Uma Belor, but not the one that Emang was supposed to be at. Lake Livan clambered out of the boat and quite unabashed deposited a pile of turds on the river bank while we unloaded.

The farmhouse was a simple two-roomed construction with banana leaves keeping out the rain. It served as a forward camp during harvesting. The evening was jolly with the bush telegraph being relayed on and being brought up to date on general news. Their ghetto-blaster radio was playing a medley of Elvis Presley songs. Guinness Stout and Elvis Presley cassettes were the two Western props which penetrated the furthest into the interior; when these two fell by the wayside blessed peace ruled.

The next day we went to look for Emang, over to the other side of the Balui and into Uma Belor, a Kayan longhouse of approximately forty doors. While the others were inquiring I went to buy some soap from a Chinese 'shop'. Most longhouses over thirty doors have a Chinese in a hut trading a few simple products and operating a motorised husk remover.

His hovel was surrounded by snorting pigs, rootling about. I walked to the open area below his room; his wife, a native woman, pointed that he was upstairs. I clambered up and was greeted by a bundle of bones lying on a mat smoking opium. He swivelled a pair of drugged eyes towards me, took a short sharp inhalation on his pipe, put it down and just stared at me. His bony limbs were covered in open sores and precariously healing scabs.

I picked up two bars of soap and he held up three fingers. I paid him and he began priming his pipe with the raw opium which he had smeared on a leaf. He transferred some more of the contents of a bottle on to the leaf and then put a little into the china bowl of his bamboo-stemmed pipe. He held a flame over the glutinous black paste, inhaled sharply a couple of times and sank back into a dreamy pose.

Directions had been given as to where we would find Emang, and we all piled into the boat again and headed upstream. Minor flirtations are easy to effect in small boats. Evasive action around logs, stopping to clean the propeller and starting off again, all produce little lurches, and this provides excuses for the boys and girls to hurriedly steady themselves with hands on each other's anatomy.

'Whoops, sorry!'

'That's all right.'

Slightly more subtle pressures when sitting close together or straining to share a small umbrella can enliven an otherwise monotonous trip.

Presently we edged into a small muddy creek, and set off on foot, crossing and recrossing a small stream. At one point the bed sparkled with a cross-section of rock which contained some mineralised quartz. I do not want to start a gold rush; the opium-puffing Chinese would have had it long ago if it were valuable. This is not to say there is no gold in Borneo, perhaps in that valley. Considerable gold mines exist in Kalimantan and new 'strikes' are frequent.

The farmhouse was a longhouse structure, but without the attention to detail of a permanent longhouse; the doors were battered and the roof in poor repair. No sign of Emang; they said he had gone fishing. I later learned that in our passage through the rapids his trading goods had somehow got left on some rocks. The river had risen overnight washing away his entire stock of goods. The bush telegraph had relayed this news on to him and he had gone off in disgust — with a girl!

With all that settled, we now started the venture proper. We reentered the Linau river and spent the rest of the day poling, unloading, reloading and dragging the boat up to a farmhouse called Uma Batu (a former longhouse) below Long Geng.

We were given melons, rice, cucumbers, and a vegetable that is a cross between a melon and a cucumber. The natives were Kenyah Badang and B.E.M. Christians. There were no drink, no cigarettes, no betel nut, no dancing. Just sing-along prayers and hymns to a strumming guitar.

Instead of returning from a long, tiring day's work and lying back with one of their 'relaxatives' and chatting, an insistent bell is rung and the people are summoned for hours of religious instruction. I watched the fervour of a girl delivering one of the several sermons. Peter the Penan, who was turning out to be the boat's joker, also watched the procedure with interest and decided that the serious atmosphere needed a little levity. He waited for the Joan of Arc to step off the podium and, intercepting her, pointed towards me with one hand while he placed the other on one of her breasts as if to guide her towards me. She slapped his arm with a horrified little shriek, whereupon he grabbed her arm, twisted it back and frog-marched her down the verandah cackling. I cannot imagine many preachers have left their pulpits quite so ignominiously. However, nobody seemed to be paying much attention. Tujok was pissing off the side of the verandah in full view of the congregation.

After three hours of service I lay down to rest, which precipitated a puzzled deputation coming over and asking, 'You are a missionary, aren't you?'

I suspected Peter the Penan had put them up to something. 'No, I'm afraid not,' I replied.

A few words were then exchanged with the current person ministering, and after a decent interval the service finished.

The personnel from our boat slept out on the verandah. If one is alone the headman always insists on providing sleeping space in his quarters, but where there are several people an area on the verandah is indicated and mats that the travellers will have brought with them are laid and one sleeps out. I enjoyed sleeping on the verandah, looking up at the coconut fronds swaying lazily to a clammy breeze and listening to the rustling of pigs and of course the complex noises of the insect population, which gradually decreases its activity during the night from its opening crescendo at dusk. As I lay musing silently on the mat, pleasantly weary after a long day's travel, the stages of falling asleep follow the slowly descending level of insect noises. Finally, when there remains only silence, one has succumbed to slumber.

Early morning fishers, carrying their jalas, or fishing nets, and people anxious to be off to their farms early, started rising about five a.m. We also made a prompt start. After a breakfast of a cucumber each we restarted the exhausting process of making our way upstream. At places where the river was very wide with small islands dotted about, we got out of the boat and pushed it over the rocks that scraped and dragged at the bottom. Two people were usually in front hauling on the long creepers. At times the rushing water was well above our waists and it was all I could do to maintain my balance on the uneven, slippery rocks below the water.

I had equipped myself with a new pair of Gurkha army boots. By midday one was ripped open in several places and hung precariously on my foot, while the other was also torn and battered. The natives were in bare feet and after observing the effects on my boots I asked to look at their feet. The sole of each foot was a third of an inch of hard callous, and more rugged than the rubber soles on my boots. I was told by a European who had once been standing with a native next to a fire that they had both smelt burning skin and on investigating had been surprised to find that the native was unknowingly standing on a piece of burning charcoal.

The most treacherous and torrential waters to negotiate are those that are narrowed by prominent rocks with a rocky bank extending into the main stream. Here the water hits the rocks causing undertows and then comes gushing round the rocks in a mighty roar. Immediately below the rock is always a slight lee of calm water.

The technique, therefore, is to hug the bank until one is immediately below one of these tricky passages and then attempt to break through the main force of the water and head diagonally across the river to the opposite bank. Usually there will be a drop in level of several feet as this mini waterfall is broken up by the force of the water surging around the rocks. The combination produces a stretch of water in the middle of the river with waves six to eight feet high, cascading spray and swirling whirlpools. Water is sucked into vacuums only to rise almost immediately when the vacuum is released.

Directly above these maelstroms of cross currents the water is calmer. Thus the risk is in bursting from behind the protective rock and heading across to the calmer stretch. If sufficient power is not generated while one is halfway across the boat slips back into the vortices hovering on the brink of the boat's precarious course.

We plunged through the spray with the little engine screaming and all of us rowing like fury in time to a chant of 'Du, Du, Du, Du.' But sometimes it was only through the Penans springing out at the closing stages and straining on the lianas that we were eased into safety.

However, as we were approaching Wong Talang, a particularly bad set of rapids, it became obvious we were not going to make it. Suddenly, as a man, acting purely through intuition, complete forward effort was transferred to emergency survival procedure. The engine was snapped down, the rowing stopped and each man leaned out of one side of the boat with his paddle extended. I had two brief seconds to envisage my camera and baggage, if not me, disappearing for ever in the whirligig behind us, before we dropped down into the thundering cauldron. We hit the first wave with a thud. I clung to the side of the boat as the water poured over us. Through the spray and waves washing over us I could see each man with the skill of a lifetime's practice maintaining balance with his outstretched paddle. In imagination it is easy to think of doing this, but in the split-second speed that things happen my first instinct was to try to steady the boat by balancing from the inside. Once engulfed in the full fury of the rapids I could see that if everybody had done this we would have been overwhelmed instantly.

However, by the others following the correct procedure we swirled down five hundred yards of hard-won river before gaining the sanctuary of the bank. Undoubtedly fatigue had something to do with it, but also it was a miscalculation on Tujok's behalf.

Following this we spent even more time unloading and reloading, sometimes two or three times in a mere few hundred yards. We also did more dragging from the bank, often involving crawling along slippery ledges six inches wide with the rapids below us and a heavy boat to pull through as well.

Some places, such as the Talang and Sekatong rapids, were so

bad that I made big detours through the jungle. At Talang it was a three hundred foot cliff, and from high up, I watched the fantastic activities of the crewmen struggling below. We stopped briefly for lunch, which consisted of boiled fish, caught with a jala while the fire was being lit, and ferns collected by Lake Livan. Prepacked rice in banana leaves we ate cold.

We continued this exhausting routine in the afternoon and by the evening I was dropping with tiredness although I had only concentrated in keeping myself and baggage up with the boat. The sun was falling fast as we passed a magnificent waterfall tumbling over one of the rockfaces, and came into sight of a small hut set up on the grassy bank behind a wide foreshore of pebbles and rocks. The little clearing surrounding the hut was a very welcome sight. Massive buttressed trees, with dangling vines, stood sombrely all around, and the impenetrable gloom of the forest was heightened by the fading light. It gave a sense of elation to feel so isolated among the denseness all around. Before unloading and preparing a fire, I removed a bottle of whisky, offered it around and in another brief ceremony awarded Bujang his Lower Boats cap in recognition of his outstanding and unflinching performance in the rapids throughout the day.

Hauling a boat upstream through rapids — a slow and laborious business.

He was thrilled with the cap, put it on his head and for the rest of our time together he never removed it.

Long Jaka is as far as a boat can get up the Linau before a gigantic waterfall at Penan Lusong. The boat was hauled high on to the river bank and left ready for the return journey.

The walk from Long Jaka to this waterfall is about three hours of treacherous bridging and almost vertical scrub-covered cliffs falling two hundred feet into the river. Lake Livan and I, as the slowest, were put in front. Lake Livan beetled along getting first exposure to the leeches which for some reason showed a preference for wriggling under his inside-out blue swimming trunks. As they attached themselves to his vitals he would give a little bunny hop, pull his trunks down and rip off the offending gentlemen.

At this stage of the trip I was unfit. After a couple of hours of the tiring terrain, fifty pounds of weight on my back and the constant distraction of bending and removing leeches, I was totally exhausted. I sat on the side of the path, my head reeling and cramps clawing at my flabby muscles. The column ploughed past. Peter, Bujang and Tukang scented home and despite huge packs, tied together with rotan frames, went streaming ahead. Peter enjoyed bullying me (no doubt because he did not get his Lower Boats cap) and every time we came to a precarious log bridge crossing a gully, he pointed down the bank and shouted authoritatively, 'You, down there,' and with a cackle went scurrying across the log. Seego, wiry and tough, kept silently padding along with his head bent down. Tujok brought up the rear. His only baggage was a sack of sweets which he was going to use for making a 'Father Christmas' entrance at the long-house. Evan, with a huge load, remained nauseatingly cocky throughout everything. It did not matter how much he had to carry or what he had to do, he retained a flippant manner. Lake Livan, with constant verbal chastisement, seemed determined to crack his jauntiness. He never succeeded, unfortunately.

Just as I was getting some feeling back into my legs and was managing to proceed at a steady pace we were faced with fording the Beraan river. If it had been deeper we could have swum across and floated the baggage across on a raft; if it had been shallow it would have been easy to wade across. Instead it was about stomach height and broken with sharply angled rocks around which the water swirled and gurgled. The easiest passage was to go from rock to rock, leaning against them with the water pouring over one, until, feeling strong enough and with the assistance of a stout pole for balance, one tried to move on to the next. It took me half an hour and I emerged thoroughly bruised, cut and thirsty. I selected a sheltered pool and drank a gallon of water.

From the Beraan the path was much easier going. The most annoying impediments are thin trailing vines with jagged little spikes notched along the stem. These dangle invisibly on the paths and continually attach themselves to whatever part of the body brushes against them first. Like fish hooks, the only way to remove them is by reversing the direction of entry.

As we pushed along in the subdued lighting created by the thick canopy of foliage a hundred feet above our heads I began to imagine I heard a large industrial complex at work. A general background roar of powerful machinery merging into a single tone as it filtered through the tangle of undergrowth and trees. We passed a big buttressed durian tree with some of the fruit lying around its base, but they were unfit to eat.

The further we walked the louder the noise grew. Soon it was evident that it was no imagination caused by tiredness. We quite suddenly emerged from the forest into a cleared area where a few banana trees grew, but mostly it was long grass, obviously played-out padi fields. With the natural muffle of the forest gone the full impact of the massive waterfall at Penan Lusong hit us. We walked along the river bank which was a hundred feet above the river, and rounding a corner we were presented with the sight of this remarkable waterfall. The river bank was level with the top of the waterfall and the height could only be estimated from the trees growing at the bottom of the cataract, which failed to reach where the water fell from. It was an extraordinary geographical fault. The ground above the water was level with the river placidly flowing along and then quite suddenly there was a dramatic drop of at least two hundred feet.

A short distance beyond the top of the waterfall the Penans had built a longhouse. It seemed dangerously close to the waterfall, but they could not recall anybody accidentally flowing over the top. Peter the Penan, Bujang and Tukang had pushed on ahead as we neared the longhouse, so that when the rearguard staggered in the entire population was all waiting for 'Father Christmas' Tujok.

Children were screaming for *gula* (sugar) and after Tujok had untied his sack and primed them with one sweet apiece to whet their appetite, he outlined the conditions for additional sweets. Two small bags costing a few cents each for one ajat, or black and white rotan basket that Inchan's mother had been making.

The Penans are the only people to make them 'commercially'. After Tujok has taken them to the coast and the Chinese shopkeeper has put on his marker, the price leaps from two bags of sweets at a few Malaysian cents each by about one thousand percent. I offered one woman money for one but she was not interested, she wanted *gula* for her howling infant. As the children were helping themselves to the bags of sweets Tujok was frantically tying knots in a sliver of rotan to keep a record of how many baskets he was due. He operated on a credit system so that they were always mortgaged to him and he thereby prevented rivals from infringing on his beat.

The strips of metal were handed over with a couple of Malaysian dollars to be forged into parangs. They were presented complete with handles and sheaths when we returned and they sell down at the coast for about fifty dollars. Additional items from the Penans were paddles, bamboo containers, animal skins and feathers, deer horns and blowpipes.

Tujok's other main trading items were salt, monosodium glutamate, hair grease, batteries for cassettes, shirts and biscuits.

On one level the trading was almost fair for it took a child about a day to eat the sweets and its mother a full day to make an ajat. This reflected their skill as the Kenyah women spend at least a week making a basket. The Penans are the least accessible of all the Borneo tribes, and seem to prefer their secluded state. They make no attempt to move nearer the towns, and resist, as far as possible, government attempts to 'civilise' them. A longhouse school at Lusong lasted only a short time because the Kayans, who are the only people whom the Penans understand in this area, refused to go back to the impossible task of teaching people who were not interested in learning the government syllabus.

I liked the Penans, for their innate security and pride in their way of life prevented them from being shy or coy. They met you on their own terms. The children did not run off screaming if you walked towards them and the adults were not always wondering what was in my baggage and whether it might be something they would like.

In addition, for the first time I had come across natives who were living according to common sense and their own customs. The men

A typical Penan basket from Long Makaba; and right, a typical Penan child, a jungle nomad.

wore a brief loin-cloth and the women just a sarong from the waist down.

Trading activity began to die down a little as night approached and a few mosquitoes began whining around. Tujok dipped his hand into his bag and produced a spray can. He gave his arms and legs a spray and offered it around. Turning to me he offered the can saying, 'Very good. Nyamok.' They were using it against mosquitoes

but on inspecting the can I read 'Hair Net Spray'. I tried to explain. My phrase-book enabled me to get out that it was for using on hair, whereupon they all squirted their hair, plus a generous whoosh on to the hairs on my chest. I gave up, and for the rest of the trip Tujok was 'setting' his arms, legs, and hair, which seemed to attract more mosquitoes than it repelled. He was always swatting and towards the end declared that his mosquito repellant was 'no good'.

The Penans are well built and taller in stature than the other natives. Their dogs are also well fed and have good coats of hair in contrast to the bones straining at the skin and bald patches of most longhouse dogs. However, their robust physical appearance is

often offset by a pallid, anaemic-looking face, produced from regular attacks of malaria. In a perverse way it adds a spiritual attraction to their physiognomy. The Penan's diet is much higher in proteins than that of other natives. Many of them ate large quantities of meat three times a day. Instead of filling up on rice they fill up on meat. Much has been written about their nomadic system suggesting that they roam around in loosely connected groups, moving quite arbitrarily. After talking to them and making further observations upstream I found that the nomadic system is based on a series of semi-permanent camp-sites near fruit trees or good fishing or hunting areas, and that they move around a particular area, staying a few weeks at each place.

A contingent of Penans had been sent back to Long Jaka to pick up the rest of the baggage and tins of petrol. A small outboard was being borrowed from the headman to continue upstream .

Before we left, a delegation led by the headman presented themselves to me and asked for a fee for travelling in their boat upriver (although they were not providing men). I referred him to Tujok who had already arranged my package tour of three weeks' travel, including my food. Tujok obviously wriggled, for presently they were back again. The amount they asked for was small, but it was easy to envisage that the further I got, the more persistent and higher their local taxes might become. After a token resistance where I feebly maintained that I had an agreement. — 'Oh, but I had an *agreement*' — I paid him and added that I was paying no more, or if I did it would be deducted from Tujok's fee. The message was relayed to Tujok who was trying to be nonchalant and chatting up a girl. He reacted to that and after a few more words of bluff they decided to stick to their agreement. After all, it was only fair that they should try it on, like the persistent borrower who is furious if he gets what he asks for because he feels he could have asked for more. They would never have forgiven themselves if they had let a white man through without trying to tap him. I suspect that Tujok put them up to it, because left to themselves the Penans are not demanding and seem keen to be merely helpful.

We had come up eight hundred feet from Belaga and the nights were noticeably cooler. The children were munching their sweets, the women started shaving off the long strips of rotan, the cocks crowed and crowed, a dog squealed as it was kicked out of the way, hushed splats sounded on the wooden boards as people emptied their mouths of spittle, Peter the Penan promenaded with a new cassette player nursed under his arm, Bujang operated a simple bellows for forging the parang blades, his cap protecting him against the sun, and the children continually ran about. All long-houses are similar with their background noises and action, but they are certainly not the same. The tone, the atmosphere, the prosperity of longhouses differ vastly within a few miles of one another, and I think much depends on the character of each headman who leads and directs his people.

They all smoke cheroots, and children start when they are about three years old. An infant of three or four years old would be wandering around with a smouldering stick trying to light its cheroot.

The longhouse at Lusong was built at government instigation, and is a rugged affair by native standards. (The government is anxious for the fluid Penan population to settle in specific areas, and hence the programmes for encouraging longhouses to be built for them.) Most of the rooms are open on two or three sides. There are no cats and as soon as it became dark, rats started running along the beams, their shadows magnified on the walls by the oil lamps. Late at night as we slept they would descend and run around the floor nibbling up any food remains. One bold one jumped on to my arm while I was dozing off. I flung it off into a pile of firewood and tried to get back to sleep.

One of the more interesing customs that some of the natives of Borneo indulge in is to place dowels of wood, rounded at the end, through holes made in their penises. However, if one asks Ibans or people on the main rivers about it they pretend to be horrified or say that nobody does it any more. At Lusong a man volunteered that he usually had one peg in, but as his wife was pregnant he had removed it.

From Lusong we made our way up the Linau river. Occasionally we would come across a man or boy crouched near the bank fishing. They were Penans and as there were no longhouses in the area they must have been attached to the smaller encampments. Whenever we ate, Tujok and Evan would disappear for twenty minutes in their boat with a jala and return with a full basket of fish. They caught fish at every throw of the net. Ferns continued to feature prominently in our diet, together with rice bought at Lusong.

At Long Abit we came across a semi-permanent encampment; approximately eight lean-tos of considerable age were grouped together and a few fruit trees were planted around, mainly banana and papaya. Tapioca is another popular plant as its roots make a quite tasty and filling dish, while its leaves are pounded and then boiled to produce a spinachy effect. The mode of eating is to take a handful of rice, squash it about in the hand to produce a congealed ball and then dip this in fish or fern soup.

There were only women and children at Long Abit as the men were off hunting. They did not seem at all surprised to see us, and again I was struck by the Penan independence in the way they received us. It was friendly, hospitable and without a trace of apology for the poor conditions. Ibans can tend to start apologising for their simple housing to a degree where one is tempted to agree with them.

Tujok hurriedly distributed his trade goods while Seego, Lake Livan, Evan and I crouched in a lean-to with the rain pouring down. The sudden change from brilliant blue-skied sunshine to dark, thundery clouds bringing a visible wall of rain across the sky never failed to impress me. About five minutes before the rain was due to fall, we covered everything up and waited resignedly for the onslaught. Then quite suddenly it would be gone, the sun would be grilling down again and everywhere steam would be rising from evaporating water.

At Long Abit I was face to face with the simplest form of hunter-gatherer existence. It was a totally tolerant and co-operative life un-hampered by severe religious restraint. Their paganism celebrates the spirits of trees and natural forms, and after being exposed to the jungle one can feel more power, sense and logic in this system than in a world based on the Old Testament. It is jokingly said that sev-

eral missionaries working among the Ibans have been converted by the people they set out to evangelise.

Uncomplicated by dependence on industrial infrastructure, they live and let live, displaying attitudes and affect-ions that Western people spend a life-time working to achieve through the burden of having to be productive and useful. The meaning of relax takes on a special significance here. To be sur-rounded by people who covet neither material nor spiritual wealth is to be enveloped in an aura of sublimity.

However, what they do covet is sugar and salt and to this end they had an active cottage industry set up to trade with Tujok and Seego. Several new knots were added to the rotan.

The course of the Linau river is through some impressive mountainous country. The great angled sides of the mountains were uniform in their dark green colouring, providing a natural base to the changing patterns and tones in the sky, blues, pinks and greys replacing each other in an endless suc-cession of intermingling sketches.

Where the Kajang river meets the Linau was a five door Penan longhouse. It was here that Tujok finally disposed of the garish plastic-framed mirror with cupids and bunches of grapes adorning the rim. For this monster he took delivery of three baskets.

Lake Livan on this quieter stretch of river had fallen into two main occupations. The first was to roll endless successions of tiny little cheroots which he smoked in half a dozen puffs. A waterproof bamboo container hung around his waist. Inside were tobacco, a

Above, a Penan from the upper Linau river.

few leaves and a two-hundred-year-old cigarette lighter. His other occupation was crapping. He would hop out of the boat where the bank was shallow and squat down in the water, his army shirt and floral stetson cutting a ridiculous figure. He had holes in his ears which he used to store spare cheroots.

Seego spoke very little, his baseball cap pulled low over his eyes as he relentlessly rowed and poled all day. Evan, under the cursing of Lake Livan, rowed, paddled and pushed harder than anybody. Tujok happily sat in the back operating the outboard while the petrol held out. When it ran out he paddled desultorily. Without the engine it was suddenly quiet and peaceful. The constant whirr had not only been an unpleasant background noise, but also frightened away the wild-life. Now without it, numbers of monkeys, pigs and birds presented themselves. The magnificent hornbills glided over the river and their harsh rattling calls in the treetops could be heard from hundreds of yards away. The big kite wheeled around the sky. This bird is used as an omen tester, in the same way as black cats crossing one's path. The natives set store by the direction of the bird's flight. Basically if it was flying in the same direction as we were heading all was okay; if not, stop work please. Fortunately I was accompanying natives in a direction that they wanted to go anyway, so that even if one of the birds had done a low level head-on swoop at us, we would have continued.

This seemed to be the general pattern. If I had hired some natives to go somewhere, omens and various 'dangers' would have been far more liable to become important, especially if we were going at a tiring pace, whereas if I was following one of their own groups somewhere, nobody paid much attention to the signs. Barking deer could make as much noise as they liked if a party was set on reaching a longhouse before nightfall.

On arrival at Long Kajang a small deputation met me, the head-man lined up some of the men, a helping hand was extended up the notched logs and I went down the line shaking hands. I expect the bush telegraph had arranged this, but it was difficult to imagine anybody could have travelled faster than we had.

A big deer had been killed that day and we had an excellent repast of venison and rice spiced with a little chili.

The population on the Linau and Kajang rivers is now very small indeed and the only natives are Penans. At one time this was a main route and natives from many tribes were living along its banks. It is difficult to imagine now. The forest sems to have completely re-grown to its original or outwardly original (conservationists would say otherwise) state.

Our mission had been going so successfully that Tujok was running short of trading items. However he had to spend at least another week upriver so the hundred-odd baskets being made at the different stops could be completed.

We continued upstream to the Penan Apoh with a very rugged longhouse near Long Tangit. They had built it only three years previously, mainly with the encouragement of some Penans from Lusong who had married into their group and described some of the advantages; but longhouse life still does not really suit the Penans. They seem to regard it as a rather unnecessary nuisance to be constantly maintaining and building refinements to an otherwise basic shelter.

As we made our final approach to their settlement Lake Livan gave a two-handed scratch to his head and, curling his hands over his eyes like binoculars, turned backwards and forwards from me to the longhouse. He had two cheroots in each of his ears, and had managed to replace his stetson the wrong way round. I got a fit of laughing which only encouraged his antics more.

Although I was the first European that most of the children, and probably some of the adults, had seen their interest was not levelled at the colour of my skin, not surprisingly as they are almost white themselves, but 'Why are your eyes blue?'. In fact a European with a tan is considerably darker than those natives who spend most of their time hunting in the shade of the jungle. The shade of skin is directly reconcilable with proximity to the coast. The Malays in the coastal towns can be very dark people and from this extreme gradually tone down to the Penans who are off-white.

A half Iban, half Penan from Lusong whose youth had coincided with the few years that there was a school there, spoke a little English and was married to one of the Penan Apoh girls. In addition he had once been hired by a Captain Bagshaw to help trap birds near Lusong and had acquired a certain military style. He placed himself in charge of me, and wanted to know if he could help in any way. I suggested collecting some of the medicinal plants and the list on the next page was the result of an enjoyable day searching around for the different types.

Some of the plants had stronger spirits than others and before picking them he dug his parang into the ground in front of them and we waited a short time while the spirit was appeased; I wondered if it was an Iban idea from his father. The really powerful spirits forbade the plant even being pointed out let alone collected unless it was to be actually used. One of them, seradon, I inadvertently discovered when I indicated an ivy-type creeper and asked its name.

Some Penan medicinal plants

No.	Penan name of plant	Habitat	Remarks
1.	Lakusebet	Open Jungle	Pound leaves and apply to wound for three days.
2.	Apujaka	Open Jungle	Seven flowers wrapped in the leaf. Cooked. Applied to septic wound.
3.	Laku Sirwelu	Open Jungle	Seven roots boiled. Drink the water. For stomach ache.
4.	Laku Bakulu	Open Jungle	Boil six inches of the stem and drink. For fever.
5.	Lakus Demen	Open Jungle	Seven roots boiled. Drink the water. For urethritis.
6.	Laku Kubaba	Open Jungle	Seven roots boiled. Hold water in mouth. For tooth-ache.
7.	Kalalay	Primary Jungle	Chew leaves to extract juice. Spit into hand. Hold for two minutes. Apply to skin rash.
8.	Talingon	Primary Jungle	Seven leaves heated. Apply to area of broken bones.

This is a selection from the twenty-two 'medicinal' plants collected at an altitude of 880 feet, near Long Tangit. As can be seen the number 'seven' plays a prominent role, and this is an Iban legacy. The effectiveness of the plants went untested, and I noticed that when Johnny suffered from an ailment he preferred to ask me for a pill rather than mix up one of the above concoctions.

I have forgotten the gentleman's name but I shall call him Johnny. In addition to providing information on the outside world to this small community, he was their self-appointed lawyer. He argued violently with Tujok (more Iban blood coming out), and demanded a high price for plant collection; I gave him his Lower Boats Choices cap instead, which he seemed happy with. However, Johnny's selfless lobbying was not without an eye for the main chance and he succeeded in infuriating himself over a clever deal that went sour.

The story starts with my slipping one of the men behind a bush to get a photograph of his palang, the wooden dowel in his penis. The man had claimed to have three of these things inserted through the head of the penis, but when I offered to pay him for a photograph and he subsequently dropped his shorts I discovered only two, although there was a mark where he had removed the third. The wooden dowels are for women's pleasure, so I inquired of his wife how she enjoyed the three pieces of wood with six ends prominent. Through two sets of translators she replied that she preferred to make love when he only had one. So I scolded the man for his vanity and reduced the fee because he only had two rather than the claimed three, and suggested he complied with his wife's wishes otherwise I would have one fitted and present myself.

'You want one? Okay.' A shout went up that I wanted one and the only effective response to the advancing 'surgeons' was to flee into the jungle.

This system of putting objects through the ends of their penises used to be fairly widespread. The Ibans in particular developed sophisticated metal or bamboo tubes so that they could change from a deer horn to a piece of wood or pig bristle according to their wives' moods.

Johnny, in the meantime, had heard what had happened, and had also spotted that I had a spare Mickey Mouse watch for trading purposes in my baggage. So after a short time he came to see me with a very stern face.

'You just break law,' he said.

'How have I done that?'

'You take picture of utang palang. Must pay fine.'

'Well, it is not your cock so what are you worried about?'

'Have to give more money.'

'Sorry, you're too late, the deal's over and finished.'

Johnny was not happy and the figure he cut in a loin-cloth wearing his cap did not help me to be serious. However his manner changed and his voice became conspiratorial. He beckoned me to his room and holding an intricately woven mat that I had previously admired, but failed to secure because he did not want to sell it at any reasonable price, whispered 'Hanwash.'

78

'Handmade? Yes, I presumed that.'

'No, no, Hanwash.'

'Hanwash, hanwash. Try, some more.'

'Hanwash,' and he pointed first at the watch I was wearing and then at my bags. The message was through; Johnny wanted the Mickey Mouse 'hanwash' in exchange for his mat.

'All right. If you throw in a couple of baskets as well.'

However, a day or two later I emerged from relieving myself in the bushes to find Johnny standing menacingly on the path. 'Hanwash no good, water get inside it.'

'Let me see.'

'Not now, before.'

'Well, show it to me when it has some water in it.'

'No, I give back to you.'

'It's still going and I'm afraid that the arrangement stands unless the headman tells me he thinks it fair to exchange back.'

Johnny went steaming off to lobby support, but everybody was aware of what had happened and told him that he had no case. He sulked for a while and then recovered. Being half Iban, he was an outsider in this small community and I suspect that this was partly the reason for his abrasive, assertive manner. For although the Penans are often noisy and garrulous in their ordinary conversations, they are seldom aggressive and their nature is gentle. They are the only Borneo tribe never to have indulged in headhunting.

During the day I found it most relaxing just to sit and watch the girls pounding the padi with their heavy poles. Sometimes there would be three women alternately thumping at the small recession in the block containing the unhusked rice. In addition to the three pummelling poles one or two women would sweep back with their feet the pieces of rice that jumped out of the hole. This was done with precision gained from constant practice. A split second divided the thumps and to have mistimed would have meant badly bruised toes.

When the men took a turn at padi bashing, they swung the pestle with their arms alone. It was only the women who pounded so that the pressure rippled down their bodies in one flowing motion. It contributed much to toning up their figures: perhaps it could be introduced into health hydros to encourage Western women to become more supple.

When we were not eating rice with ferns, we had tropical fruit, which however tended to go rotten very soon after it was picked. In order to avoid this happening to the bananas, they would pick them when they were young and hard and then boiled them. This completely eliminated all taste, which made them dull eating. Tujok and Evan caught fish to supplement this diet and to provide our share of food towards the rest of the community.

One morning Lake Livan came and nudged me, making his binocular gesture and pointing towards the bank. I collected my camera and found some men manhandling a huge boar weighing at least two hundred and fifty pounds, with great curved tusks over eight inches long. The boar was then shared out between everyone, which seemed to be the custom with all game brought in. Without a fridge, one family could not hope to eat the vast quantities of meat on a large jungle animal before it began to deteriorate so I soon became as familiar with boiled boar as with fern soup. In the over-hunted coastal areas a babi or pig is considered a great delicacy and a few pieces are shared out but here in the hinterland huge bowls were filled with chunks of the meat and dished out to everyone. We would sit round in different rooms chewing at these hunks of pork, whilst Lake Livan would give his head the usual two-handed scratch and place his stetson the wrong way round before he began to eat.

The night before we left a dance was arranged. The Penans seemed to copy Kayan dancing and did it very well. Tujok acquitted himself well with a technically perfect performance that drew an appreciative response from the audience. Lake Livan sat alternating between binocular gestures and rolling cheroots.

The Penan men have developed their own dance which is halfway between the uncontrolled Iban capering and the strict form of the Kayans and Kenyahs. A drum starts a rhythm, another one joins in with a slightly different beat and on to the floor prances a man imitating a monkey or some other animal. It draws laughs from the crowd but it is performed with a definite pattern in mind. One half of the body seems to maintain one of the drums' rhythms while the legs danced to the other. It seemed more African than Asian.

The morning we left a dog had drowned at the spot where they washed and collected water. It didn't seem to worry them. The corpse was already swelling in the heat and drinking water was being collected as usual from just below the corpse. When we finally left at mid-morning the corpse was still there. Perhaps they would wait for the river to rise and wash it away.

I asked what generally happened to dogs when they could not hunt. The Kayans had told me they tied a stone round its neck and threw it in the river, but the Penans were much kinder to their dogs. I often saw them petting them, and they did not slink out of the way when one approached, as most of the dogs do, expecting a hefty boot if they do not move; and it seemed that their old dogs drown the day that they are too weak to make it across a swollen stream. The number of dogs at Penan Apoh was about sixty against roughly fifty people. At least half these dogs were unsuitable for hunting purposes, and at times there was hardly room to sit down as the dogs had bagged all the room. I felt there was some justification in the more drastic action of the Kayans.

Our planned route had been to go up the Tangit river as far as possible and then walk for a day to Penan Busang on the Kajang river, a twenty-door longhouse. However, so successful had been the demand on Tujok's supplies that there was nothing left to take, so we started back down the river.

With no engine and a tired crew we relied on the stream to carry us down, occasionally dipping oars to keep the boat straight and in the middle of the stream. It was a memorable trip, the burning, bright heat reflected from the river, dappled a little by the shadows and deep colours of the foliage lining the banks. Nobody spoke much while it was hot; all that disturbed the stillness was the occasional ripple, from a paddle, or from a fish surfacing to snatch at a fly or berry with a little 'tock' sound as it disappeared in the water. Far up these rivers the atmosphere is quite different from the lower reaches. The air is lighter and less stifling, mountains rise up in the background or sometimes from the banks of the river itself. Land is cleared only immediately around the tiny communities; the stretches in between contained massive walls of trees, giant fronds and dangling creepers.

An exhilarating sensation of freedom is inescapable, surrounded by unexploited nature as far as the eye can see. The significance of the monumental drawbacks in living in such an environment confront one squarely, but still they fail to detract from the soul-stirring serenity of the scene. A longing to exist in a form of suspended animation, bathing in the warmth of the sun and coolness of the water, forever floating downstream in a landscape of complete harmony, enveloped me as our boat drifted silently along. The hours flicked drowsily by in pleasant meditation, and never did I find the day too long or uncomfortable while travelling downstream by canoe.

At Long Kajang where the Kajang river joins the Linau I was given the head of a rhinoceros hornbill. We had, of course, stayed there on our way up and coming back they treated us like old friends. In such a remote place, to see somebody twice is enough to class him or her as your friend.

Slowly and easily we went back down the river that had provided such an effort to come up. We were still above the Lusong waterfall where the river takes such a dramatic downward course. If we

stayed a night on the bank we would stop where a native had built a simple lean-to and strengthen it with some new pieces of wood; and being a party of traders drape a waterproof tarpaulin over the framework instead of large leaves.

The group of Penans at Long Abit had not finished their baskets so we stayed a day while they completed them. Then we raced on trying to reach Lusong before nightfall. Six o'clock came and the sun began its rapid descent. A superb sunset gave us something to admire as we all took turns paddling the boat. At seven thirty the regular nightly rain started and quickly developed into a thunderstorm. Huge jagged flashes of lightning lingered across the sky like the stylished storms in old black and white horror films. The rain pummelled down, creating such a noise that I was worried that we might miss the longhouse set back from the river, and go toppling over the waterfall.

On and on we paddled; the storm cleared but the rain continued. The sky was pitch black with the clouds covering the moon so that there was no reflection at all on the water. It was impossible to see which way the river curved and to follow the shortest route.

Eight o'clock, nine o'clock, ten o'clock, passed and we all began to get tired; this was not the pleasant downstream cruise I had been enjoying during the day. Finally at quarter to eleven we sighted a few pencils of light showing through the cracks of the longhouse from the small oil lamps. They were scarcely visible, but the roar of the waterfall told us where to look.

The heavy rain had caused flooding and we waded through water up to our thighs, scrambled up the notched logs and keeled over on to our mats to sleep soundly until dawn.

The next day the big count up started. How many baskets, parangs and paddles had the local people completed? Not as many as Tujok wanted, so he decided to stay a little longer to collect more. He would leave when they still owed him some; a business technique he had learned from the Chinese I expect.

I noticed that the room we had stayed in on the way up was completely devoid of any personal possessions. The Penan family had gone off somewhere, and left no trace of their identity. It seemed to suggest that the longhouse, built at the instigation of the government, was used merely as another transit stop on their rounds through the jungle.

One cannot emphasise enough the difference between the Penans

Penan mothers with their children, including babies in bark and rotan carriers. This picture was taken in the upper Baram valley.

and all other Borneo natives. The Penans are jungle dwellers whereas the rest are riverine people with farms, living a rural life enjoyed by millions of smallholders the world over. Their skill in the jungle is limited, they very rarely travel any distance from the longhouse on their own and are full of stories about the pitfalls waiting for the unwary traveller. The Penans are completely the reverse. They feel secure slipping through the tangled undergrowth and between the majestic trunks of the towering trees. They quite happily set off on long journeys alone and are never at a loss to find something to eat, or the way to cross a natural barrier. They share none of the panicky apprenhension of getting lost in the jungle that characterises the others.

The Penans I saw on the Linau were followers of Bungan, the religion mentioned earlier.

Many of the people at Lusong whom I had seen earlier had gone to collect rotan for making baskets. The variety of this long creeperlike plant suitable for making baskets is usually found in well established areas, often quite far from the site of the longhouse. To the connoisseur, the quality of rotan is immediately obvious.

While Tujok sat around waiting for his goods to be ready I accompanied a native on a blowpiping hunt into the jungle. We kept off the paths, and, but for me, would have been silently slipping through the forest in expectation of surprising an unwary monkey or bird. After a couple of hours with the Penan hunched like a creeping cat, finger covering a dart in readiness up the end of the blowpipe, I could see that my presence was hindering the hunt. He indicated that we should sit in a slightly open area with a good view of the surrounding trees.

Presently a bird alighted on one of the trees. I had seen it swoop in, but then lost it. However the Penan raised his pipe, holding it right at the end with his hands clasped underneath, quickly sighted the bird and puffed so silently I heard nothing.

He turned and smiled, and although I could still see nothing, he indicated a hit. We waited about five minutes during which time a ruffling in the tree revealed the bird's position. It began to sway drunkenly and then came tumbling down. It had been about fifty feet up, and had been shot straight through the neck. The poison tip of the dart had gone clean through it so that it had not had a chance to work on the bird, which was small and green, with a wingspan of about six inches. On the way back, to demonstrate the power of his pipe, he shot a dart through a banana stem eight inches thick.

The following day great excitement was expected; the downriver radio station had announced that the flying doctor was to visit

Lusong. Although it was scheduled to visit once every three months (for an hour) it had not called for six months.

The irregularity of this service is due to emergency calls from bush clinics upsetting the schedule, and also the habit of politicians and businessmen chartering the flying doctor's helicopter for their own purposes. They prefer to do this because the rate of charter is much lower from the flying doctor than from the government heli- copters. The result is obviously to the detriment of the people for whom the helicopter was intended.

I had begun to take an interest in the medical facilities of the nat- ives, because their traditional medicinal remedies have been so ridiculed by outsiders that they have very nearly died out. A patient would be left to get worse and worse in the hope that the flying doc- tor would come soon. It needs little imagination to realise that with such an irregular service most illnesses have begun, run their course and finished off their victims long before the doctor appears. It was additionally enlightening to see what happened when the doctor did finally arrive. The helicopter came whirring in and everybody crowded round. The children were swatted off by an irate pilot who, understandably, was fed up with having his glass dome covered in muddy fingers. The doctor, accompanied by three nurses, strode along some new bridging prepared for the visit and set about their work. The nurses vaccinated new-born children while the doctor attempted to treat a throng of babbling patients, and everybody from the longhouse jostled each other in tight circle round the doctor.

I spoke to the pilot who said it was the same everywhere. As it was quite impossible to make any detailed examinations, it merely en- abled those people who were fortunate enough to be at death's door when the doctor visited their longhouses to be flown to the hospital at Kapit. The rest had to manage on their own.

Simple medicines were handed around to the first fifteen in the queue, and then twenty-five minutes after arriving, the medical team packed up and went flying away. I had mentioned to the doc- tor that there was a very sick man in Long Dupar, and she stated that she would go there the next day to see him.

Returning to my adopted position on the verandah I noticed a mother returning from the melee with her child who had got an appalling scourge of impetigo, or worse, all over her body.

'Did you get some medicine?' I asked her.

'No,' she replied. 'The doctor didn't have time to see her.'

While talking to the pilot I asked about giving lifts when the heli- copter was not full.

'I have no objections at all, but there can be problems.'

'In what way?'

'Well the other day I met a Dutchman with a big bushy beard and a sketch pad who asked me to give him a lift to wherever I was going. As I was going to a very remote longhouse, and there was room in the helicopter I dropped him off there. I've no idea how he'll get back. A couple of days later I was telling somebody about it and the Resident overheard and was furious. He summoned me to his office, told me he wanted to see the Dutchman, and didn't I know that he had been dropped off in a military area.'

'So what happened?'

'Nothing. I told the Resident that when there were written regulations I would comply; but they won't write them because it would also affect them chartering the helicopter.'

It was an amusing follow-up to the Dutchman's fortunes. I imagined that the flight had eluded his Kayan wife; well, now he had justified the nickname for him in Belaga of 'The Flying Dutchman'. The pilot went on to tell me how he broke the boredom of endlessly flying to different stations.

'When there's nobody on board I fly along the rivers at about fifty feet, banking round the corners; when the natives see me coming they dive out of their boats into the water. It's quite safe unless I meet another helicopter doing the same thing coming from the other direction.'

Our final night at Lusong was marked by an entertainment of animal dances and pulsating drums. While this was going on Lake Livan was crouched over a skin which he was laboriously stretching over a frame. We had earlier dined on this cat-like creature the size of a fox which had the toughest, stringiest meat I have ever eaten. It did not affect the others who, observing my difficulty, would merely repeat, 'Bagus, bagus. (Good, good).'

The walk back to Long Jaka was much less tiring. The spartan diet and extra exercise were having a beneficial effect, and I was surprised at how well I felt. We picked up our own canoe again, and then travelled down the river from Long Jaka to Long Linau in about a quarter of the time it took to go up. The boat was eased into the centre of stream where rushing, boiling water took hold of us and sped us away like a piece of flotsam in a snow avalanche. The skill required now was to ensure that the boat did not hit any rocks and that our course took us through the quietest waters. This was not easy. Once in a surging current it was difficult to break out of it.

Several times we had to unload the boat, carrying down the goods and then guiding the boat close to the bank.

At Long Talang we tried to bring the boat to the bank but the flow was too strong for us. A huge wall of water appeared. There was time only for a quick prayer as the inevitable confrontation loomed upon us. Seego, sitting up high in the bows with a rod to try to fend off rocks, disappeared into the wave first. and was thrown on his back at the bottom of the boat. Lake Livan was awash next and his floral stetson went flying past me as the water smashed over the rest of us. We began baling frantically as we only had about two inches of free-board and the next onslaught was a short way ahead. Only by an all-out effort from everybody did we remove sufficient water in time to face the next bad patch. Much shouting, most of it useless, accompanied the continual process of baling out water and desperately manoeuvring the boat to face the next vortex of waves.

When we finally reached the calm of the Balui our arms, legs and backs were aching in every muscle from the non-stop effort in keeping the boat afloat. It was not only hard work, it was also exciting and exhilarating. The sense of achievement in bringing the boat safely down, the part that everybody had played, gave us a pleasant camaraderie and added an edge of nostalgia to the prospect of presently reaching 'home' at Tujok's longhouse. The profits made by Tujok were high, but how many people were prepared to labour on such a trip every so often, risking life and property?

In the evening we celebrated our return with borak while some girls did a dance for us. I had now stayed at this longhouse on three occasions and having completed a trip with their headman I was accepted by the people there, which made it especially friendly. Tujok in a generous gesture voluntarily reduced the 'package' fee he had charged me.

7

Back to Long Jawi

I returned downstream to Belaga where I met Emang and found out why he had not accompanied us. Up until then I had not realised his absence was due to his goods being lost at the Bakun rapids. He was disappointed that he had not been able to use his leave in making this trip as planned, especially as the Penans understand Kayan, and he wanted to find out as much about them as possible in line with his work. I was sorry too as I would have learned more had I had somebody who could have translated for me.

My next intention was to go back up the Balui, past Long Jawi, over the Indonesian border to Long Nawang in Kalimantan and then probably down the Mahakam river. I told Emang my plans and also mentioned the delightful Inchan at Long Jawi. 'What would be a suitable present to give her, in view of the hospitality she has shown?' I asked Emang.

He thought for a while and came up with a gong and a sarong. I realised he was playing me along a little, as these two items mark a betrothal; but entering into the spirit of his plan we made enquiries in the bazaar for the two items. A sarong was easy, but a gong was more difficult. As highly prized heirlooms in native society, the gongs have prices inflated to their proper value and I was unable to secure one at a price I could afford.

Further enquiries in the bazaar revealed a timber boat proceeding in the right direction the following morning. We left at about six o'clock with an enormous load of sawn timber which affected the steering adversely. The boat was about thirty-five feet long and made of iron. On board were a Kenyah woman, two Kayans, myself and a crew of three typical up-river Chinese: muscular, noisy, confident and incessantly gambling.

We struggled along against the current but at the rapids just below Long Linau an incident occurred which I had often wondered about: what happens when a longboat is struggling up the negotiable passage of a rapid and another boat comes zooming down? I had my answer here, for a longboat full of children and piloted by a harassed native suddenly emerged on a straight collision course with us.

Our pilot waved him out of the way, just as a truck or bus driver might continue a hazardous overtaking when the on-coming vehicle is a mini. The longboat had no choice but to steer into a menacingly rough patch of water on our left. I caught a glimpse of the wide-eyed horror of the children as their boat disappeared into the waves to re-emerge a second or two later, instantly steering back to the easier passage while the children started baling water. Fortunately they had a proper sized engine in relation to the size of their boat and were able to recover their course immediately.

Our boat churned on. It was disconcerting to watch the Chinese pilot confidently making jokes in his staccato language while turning the wheel several twists of the old chain connected to the rudder and then waiting a few moments before the boat responded.

As the afternoon sun beat down we saw ahead of us two fishermen with their nets spread across a section of the river. The floats marking the location of the nets were clearly visible, but either the pilot was not concentrating or the boat was not turning, and we succeeded in churning straight through their nets. The natives looked on with horrified, murderous expressions, and in a very ungenerous gesture our boat continued on its way.

However, a short distance further on, the level of the river was so low that we were unable to proceed with safety. One of the crew was perched on the front of the boat sounding the bottom with a rod. It was a hopeless prospect so they decided to return to Long Liko to wait for the water level to rise.

The scene at Long Liko soon after we arrived was in the best tradition of natural comedy. The swaggering boatmen tied up their vessel, checked the propellor for remains of the net and were generally throwing their weight around, when from behind a coconut tree stepped a couple of natives with grim features carrying the remains of their fishing net.

In half a second flat the boatmen's smugness had dissolved in a revolting display of obsequiousness. Their hands got tangled in their pockets in their haste to pull out their money. A price was agreed, Chinese arms round native shoulders, wide grinning mouths of gold teeth and no doubt a few 'phews', and the matter was settled.

I had delayed on the boat to watch the scene, but now with peace restored, approached the longhouse. On entering a Kayan longhouse it is customary to say *'Haman ma'un uma?'* which simply means, 'Is there a taboo in force?' In order not to be put in the embarrassing position of being told there is, a custom has been developed whereby two crossed paddles with a hat hanging on top are placed prominently on the river bank to indicate when a longhouse is under taboo. Similarly if a particular room is under taboo a hat is hung on the outside of the door.

Having approached in the prescribed way, the reception on entering can vary enormously. Kayans on the Balui in particular are split in their attitude to Europeans. This follows a great expedition led by Rajah Charles Brooke in 1863 where with a force of Ibans he soundly defeated a very gallant army of Kayans, and pushed them back from Long Pila above the Pelagus rapids to Belaga. This also marked the changing of the name of the river. Balui is a Kayan word and before 1863 the Balui stopped at Long Pila, now it stops where the Belaga river joins the Rajang. The pretext for attacking the Kayans was that they had harboured the murderers of two of the Rajah's officers, called Fox and Steele, at Kanowit.

It is interesting how fresh in the mind of the Kayans this event is. On reflection it does not seem surprising. They have fairly uneventful lives; and a major battle as in 1863 where they lost their sovereignty and vast tracts of hard-won land acquired over a very long period must be the equivalent for them of the two world wars rolled into one for Germany.

It can be seen therefore that a Kayan community that was previously based downriver and is now located further back, will almost certainly harbour a traditional grudge against the European.

Fortunately Long Liko was not one of these. An elderly gentleman, grinning wickedly, shook me warmly by the hand and without releasing it led me down to where his family was, introduced them all to me, gave a nod and wink towards his attractive granddaughter and proceeded to take me upstairs.

Some fruit was brought up by the grand-daughter and some of her friends. As I recall it was the delicious rambutan and mata kuching. Fortunately his grand-daughter, called Minna, could speak some English as she had gone to school in Belaga. I never failed to be amazed at the proficiency native people showed in languages. A few months learning English in a small school, taught by another native, never being able to practise with English-speaking people, they nevertheless could understand and speak extremely well. It is still a point of prestige to be able to speak English and they work hard at it. The Malaysian government, however, is trying to phase down the extent to which English is used, in favour of their own developing Bahasa Malaysia. The Chinese wisely stayed on board their craft for the night and boiled up some noodles while I was being royally entertained with rice, scrambled egg with onion, boiled tapioca leaf and fern, and durian, followed by coffee.

Later some other girls came up to teach me more Kayan words, while all the men chewed betel nut and puffed on their cheroots downstairs. Lights out time came and Minna with another young girl lay down on a mat. I positioned my mat nearby but obviously too close, because after a while her mother came up to inspect the scene and obviously did not approve. She sent the old grandfather up to chaperone the girls. He did not seem very interested and placed himself at the far end of the room, but then positioned the oil lamp so that the girls and I were well illuminated. He sat on his mat, unrolled his betel nut equipment, and like a contented cow chewing the cud, gazed into space with slowly masticating jaws.

It rained during the night which brought the river up to a passable level, so the Chinese sent a boy up to tell me they were leaving.

The crew were more subdued than the previous day. They needed to concentrate on the river that had risen so much that it was now tricky to navigate the overloaded boat. Pieces of flotsam from longhouses such as notched logs that had broken loose, old tree trunks washed from the banks where they had fallen, and the occasional dead dog came floating past on the swollen stream. It is these downpours that do so much damage to areas that have been cleared for farms or timber. Within minutes an area that is unprotected by a canopy of trees can have tons of top-soil washed away into the rivers. This leaves a barren piece of ground and results in big mud banks building up on some of the river curves.

Hour after hour the pilot steered a commendable course around rocks and avoided the bobbing tree trunks that came ponderously down on the main current. Slowly they would appear above the surface of the water like water serpents raising their heads for air, before hitting an eddy in the river that sucked them down for a few moments and then back up they would come in some different position. It needed constant vigilance to avoid ramming these hazards.

I suspect it was partly the culmination of taking evasive action from a log, and partly a misjudgment in steering a close course to the rocks in the rapids above Uma Juman that precipitated a near disaster.

The boat was being lurched around the river by the jolting undertow, steering extremely arbitrarily, when I noticed that under no circumstance would we be able to alter course in time to avoid a large rock outcrop. The pilot had swung the wheel as far as it would go, and was applying all his weight to the wheel so that the chain connected to the rudder was vibrating with the force of his desperate gesture.

The native woman was lying longways on a pile of wood, while the little native man sat on the inside steps of the craft like a mesmerised rabbit. He seemed unable to visualise the effect of the boat graunching into the rocks. I dived longways and hung on to the boat's metal frame. At the last second the pilot realised a collision was unavoidable and cut power, but it was far too late. He had not even managed to make it a glancing blow; we rammed head on into the rocks with a tremendous crunching of metal and rock working on one another. The crouching native was catapulted like a rag doll into the boat's superstructure and flopped back across the steps, where he lay draped, with blood oozing from a head wound.

The collision precipitated a rock fall on to the front of the boat which smashed the front of the cabin and completely cut the pilot's visibility. A mass of rock was piled on to the front. The native woman, who had been unaware that anything was going to happen, slid forward on impact and collected a few splinters.

However, we were still in a rapid and there was no time to assess damage. The crew hurriedly cleared a space so that the pilot could see, while the boat wallowed backwards. With view regained, power was increased, and we made for the nearest calm bay where the clearing-up started. A noisy post mortem took place on the reasons for the accident.

The native was given some tea and sticking plaster and was harangued by the Chinese for being in a 'dangerous position'. An argument broke out among the Chinese, which seemed to revolve around the guilty pilot insisting on 'having another go'. Eventually he was sent back to work the bilges and tinker with the engine. The boat, surprisingly, was not badly dented and so I presume it had been reinforced against just this type of collision.

The native woman was busy picking splinters out of her tattooed legs, an operation which enabled me to see the extent to which they tattoo. The highest rings were at the top of her thighs, which seemed a waste of effort, for who could then admire the intricate handiwork of the tattooist? I asked her and she said it was for the gods to admire. This seemed unsatisfactory, and it was not until I met Kenyah women in Kalimantan with the same tattoos, who instead of wearing sarongs had either loin-cloths or brief aprons hitched up at the sides so that the tattoos were exposed for all to admire, that I understood why the markings went so high.

When we reached Rumah Daro at Long Benalui the crew decided to carry out a proper inspection, and repair some of the super-structure. This activity meant that we stayed the night here.

Rumah Daro was the scene of my dog despatching act; and I was therefore somewhat surprised when after the evening meal I was asked to preach to the longhouse. The man asking me was most in-sistent, and put it in the terms of 'My people know nothing, they call themselves Christians but they have no idea what it means. You would be helping us greatly if you could explain.'

Presently I emerged from the headman's quarters to find the whole longhouse gathered for instruction. My choice was now elim-inated. The man who had asked me was acting as translator, and at times he appeared to be using me to put across his own points and message. I would say a couple of mild sentences, and he would launch into five minutes of invective. He cannot have been too far off the point as I regularly brought in passages of the Bible to be read aloud. The experience was interesting, and I could see how easily a rabble-rouser could operate. Everybody hung on my (or his) words with wide-eyed, believing faces. One of the techniques that the Chinese communists use to persuade the Ibans to join their cause is to pretend that they are being supported by the British. This used to be very effective, but now the word has generally filtered around that the two are not connected.

Long Bulan was our destination and the next day when we reached it, the woman kindly suggested I stay with her family. The longhouse was about sixty-five doors altogether and divided by a small river. The verandah was about twenty feet wide and thirty feet high. The rooms were enormous.

As soon as we arrived, an imbecile came slobbering and gibber-ing to where we were unloading. He was a herald for a series of cripples and mentally retarded people wandering or sitting about in the public area. It was the first time I had seen so many at a long-house and in public. Earlier brushes with abnormalities had usu-ally been in the confines of a family room; indeed one young man, who was prone to violence, had been kept in a cage-like cell adjoin-ing the back of the longhouse.

An albino I saw was treated like anybody else and mental der-angements did not seem to be treated on a superstitious level. It seemed a humane system to have the mentally sick living freely in the community and being treated, as far as it was possible, like anybody else. I have often wondered since why there were so many deformities and deficiencies at Long Bulan; perhaps some obscure disease was responsible.

To add to this confusion native pastors had been at work and the longhouse was divided between Bungan, Roman Catholic and a single Muslim family (the woman I was staying with).

Nothing highlights religious doctrine more than to find two or three religions at close quarters being devoutly adhered to by people from the same families. Catholic priests remain celibate but can drink and smoke; B.E.M. priests can get married, but must not drink or smoke. I often heard somebody's reason for choosing a particular religion based solely on these factors.

In the course of conversations, I discovered that the woman with whom I was staying was going to Long Nawang in Kalimantan. This seemed an excellent chance for me to follow and she willingly agreed that I could do so. She was accompanying some Indonesian Kenyahs who had already set off paddling upstream. This did not worry her as there was bound to be a motor-powered boat that could be waved into the bank, that was going on to Long Jawi or Long Busang.

Sure enough a small boat with an outboard came putting along two days later and we made our way to Long Jawi.

My spirits were high when we arrived, for now I felt certain of getting through to Indonesia. This would require guides and porters to carry the boat over the hills on the border, to the stream in Kalimantan, but I was relieved of the uncertainly of finding people who might not be going for a week, two weeks or more, or having to hire a whole party on my own count.

I walked with a light step into the penghulu's quarters and nearly crumpled at the knees when ranged along the raised platform was the district officer, the police sergeant in charge of the area and assorted soldiers toting machine guns.

After putting down my bags I ambled through to the cooking quarters at the back. I had hardly sat down when one of the soldiers came through, and waggled his gun from me to the other room. The message was clear, the district officer requested an interview.

The district officer was a Malay and his entourage were also Malays. Their expedition was going to Long Busang to promote Islam among the people there. Local people explained to me the methods range from being offered land 'rights' (i.e. being issued with a birth certificate), to free loans to buy agricultural equipment, to a special dispensation — native Muslims can eat pig.

The district officer told me, 'The Kayans and Kenyahs are primitive people, they are not yet ready to be subjected to visits from Europeans. They have got to be civilised slowly, so I'm afraid you will have to return downriver.'

While he said this a Kenyah man, who spoke better English than the district officer, sat and listened with a bland smile on his face. 'Don't you think a little cultural interchange is a good idea?' I tried on the district officer.

He changed tack and said, 'I am not able to discuss my views, and although I can't order you down the police sergeant can.'

This prompted the police sergeant to weigh in next, telling me that 'Action would be taken if I went further upstream', and that I must return on the first available boat.

When they were ready they left upriver for Long Busang. I lay down and debated with myself whether it was worth going on or not. If I tried going on upriver I almost certainly would bump into the D.O.'s party again, and may be land myself in trouble. While in my deliberations a knot of schoolchildren came bustling in babbling about Inchan. I had completely forgotten her. So as some welcome light relief I unpacked the sarong I had brought for her and sent it along with one of the children.

In the next two days the only boat to arrive was a Chinese trader on his way upstream. I was sorely tempted to go on with him, but the deciding factor was the ludicrous price he was trying to charge.

In the evening there was a brief respite for my frustrations. A 'kanjet' was organised at one of the longhouses. I arrived as the girls were in the middle of the long dance. About fifteen of them were going through a complicated routine that was a joy to watch. I do not think I have ever seen such a collection of pretty girls before. Long Jawi has about sixty unmarried girls and only about twenty bachelors. The imbalance has been produced by the boys going down to the coast to look for jobs.

The following day was Saturday, and was marked by a long B.E.M. religious service. It started late in the afternoon on the large porch outside the penghulu's quarters. Hymns, sermons and prayers continued in rotation hour after hour. The congregation was fairly fluid; people drifted in and out according to when they had the time. They sang several well known hymns; using their own words of course, but the tune was always steady and the gusto they put into it was something unknown to the average poorly attended parish church in England. I remember particularly their rendition of *My Song is Love Unknown*, which was beautifully sung. The mellow tropical night, with a background of palm trees and buzzing insects, seemed a most fitting setting for this sober melody.

I lay down to sleep with the service still in progress and the following morning I awoke to find it still going on. I never asked whether it had continued all night or just started again early in the morning.

Another B.E.M. tenet is that nobody must do any work on Sundays. This seemed a mixed blessing, especially during harvest time. Some people used this forced day off to drink illicit borak in their rooms.

A football game was arranged in the afternoon which was attended with about as much keenness as football supporters show in England. Barefooted players raced about displaying highly skilful play.

In Brunei I once watched a seven-a-side rugger tournament organised by the large expatriate oil company community. Several native teams took part and the highlight of the tournament was a barefoot team of natives from Kuching with nobody taller than five feet four inches beating a hulking, well trained European team.

At Long Jawi, however, it was football, and closely-fitting skull caps made of tightly woven rotan were a great help in heading the ball. A winger who had been having a quiet game disappeared at one point into a group of rushes to relieve himself. Moments later a wild, high kick sent the ball plummeting towards the rushes. It momentarily disappeared, and following a sharp groan, like somebody being coshed, the ball miraculously bounced out again. The man relieving himself had executed an unintentional header, about the only time he had touched the ball. The crowd roared with laughter and two people entered the rushes to bring out the dazed star.

The routine of the women generally seemed to be to work on the farm and in the house on alternate days. The men go out every day, and the children start to act as nannies when they are six or seven, looking after the younger children while their parents, older brothers and sisters are at work.

In large communities such as at Long Jawi there are craftsmen who do not work on the farms, but spend their time carving bone handles for parangs, or decorating parang blades or making blowpipes. There was one old man who specialised in decorating parangs, and executing the detailed Kenyah designs out of bone. This type of work is dying out fast despite a good demand for the products on the coast.

I had been at Long Jawi a few days and there had been no sign of any boats. The district officer and his party reappeared and suggested giving me a lift back, but I declined on principle and said I would

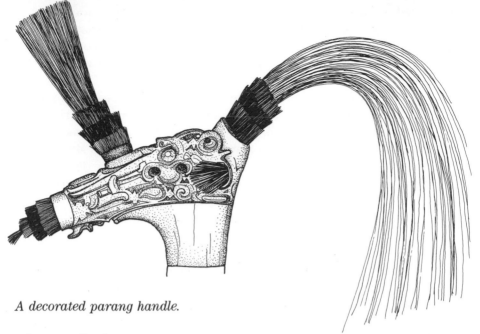

A decorated parang handle.

take a smaller boat.

I still had half a mind to carry on, but the woman whom I was to follow had already left for Indonesia. I was almost certain to be stuck in Long Busang arranging my onward journey at a time when I would want to move quickly; so when another government boat from the Public Works Department arrived I decided to go back with it. By coincidence the River Queen also arrived, and I watched as a large deer was coaxed and manhandled on board. It jumped out on the first attempt and nearly got swept away; only the rope round its neck, and its own struggles brought it panting back up the bank. Deer are sold as pets downriver, and if caught young enough make attractive and affectionate ones. Like deer elsewhere they have large 'valves' in a two inch line from the corners of their eyes. I asked several people about this. The natives call them night eyes, whereas somebody suggested they were to draw in extra oxygen when they were running and tired, but this of course is impossible.

The Public Works Department boat was under the command of a pleasant, bespectacled Melanau official. He seemed to have a very large retinue for a relatively simple mission. He had come to invest-igate the possibilities of erecting some buildings that various people had deemed necessary. In addition to the rolls of plans he had a con-struction adviser, a very effeminate Muslim storeman called Ahmed who did nothing except arrange his hair and complain about the lack of cigarettes; an outboard engine mechanic who had already failed to repair the two engines that had broken (there was just one left); a boat driver; an assistant known as 'Radio' because he never stopped talking; a surly little Malay trader who had come for the ride; and a fat jovial Kenyah who came from Long Jawi. My inclusion hardly caused a ripple.

The boat only had one engine working, and to lessen the risk of this one breaking down we made rather slow progress. The boat driver was a Kayan from Batukelau (or Montecarlau as Ahmed called it), so it came as little surprise that a mile or two short of his home the last engine started spluttering ominously. Then, naturally, as the longhouse hove into view the engine died completely. The official had been anxious to go quite some distance further but to retain the initiative he announced that we would stay here the night.

The boat driver now had a night with his family, and the next morning the engines were back in operation. On the way down we stopped at Rumah Juman located at Long Dupar. This was the longhouse I had been stuck at before, and where the man with a septic knee was waiting for the attentions of the flying doctor. I asked how he was, but he had just died. I asked if the flying doctor had visited, remembering how they had promised to go the next day from Lusong. No, they had not. It was a completely unnecessary death. A young man who merely required penicillin.

When I got back to Belaga I met the flying doctor again and after discussing this case, I asked why they did not train up a representative from each longhouse to the standard of a medical dresser, thereby increasing efficiency and saving enormous cost. The categoric reason was that drugs could not be dispensed to medical dressers for treating their own people. She implied that the system would quickly be abused.

'Had they tried it?'

'No, we don't need to.'

Much later when I was lunching with a government minister I described what I had seen on the medical front in the interior, and again put forward my remedy. He thought it an excellent suggestion, marvelled that it had not been thought of before, and in true political style, pledged to do something about it. This discussion for some reason prompted him to remark on a strange character he had just met far up the Baram.

'I flew there in a helicopter to see the local people and found a European trying to get downriver.'

'Did he have a ginger beard and a sketch pad?'

98

'Yes, as a matter of fact he did, and he was Dutch.'

'Did you give him a lift?'

'No, I left him up there.'

'Do you know who he was?'

'No.'

'That was the Flying Dutchman.'

'Oh, well he didn't fly with me.'

There are several persistent features in the interior wherever you go. One is certainly the Flying Dutchman, but the most widespread is the question, 'Where are you going?' I learned to say 'For a little walk' in all the native dialects I came into contact with. This did not satisfy one fellow in Long Jawi who was anxious to know exactly where I would be going from Long Jawi; on reflex to the pumping I replied I was going to the moon next. He took it quite seriously, asked how many days it would take, how many shirts I needed, was it cold and so on. It went so far I was unable to tell him I was joking, and the morning I left I saw him standing thoughtfully on the bank, with his blowpipe over his shoulder, wondering whether to try to join me on my flight to the moon.

In Belaga I stayed with Emang, who sympathised with my aborted plans, but did not seem surprised. The express boat ride from Belaga was highly uncomfortable. It was the durian fruit season and all the way down, especially near the Punan longhouses, baskets of it were loaded into the boat until finally, through lack of room I jumped off at an Iban longhouse near the Pelagus rapids where I had once stayed before.

My original plan had been to go east into Kalimantan up the Balui or Kajang rivers but I had been baulked. Now I would try another way. I would fly up to Bario in the Kelabit Highlands in northeast Sarawak and see if I could walk across the border unobserved from there. This would turn out to be a more interesting, if more tiring, route.

8

The Kelabit Highlands

The flight to Bario is on a Norman Islander, and the seat bookings are rather arbitrary. To ring Miri airline office is invariably to be told that the flight is full for the next two weeks, but to turn up at the airport is usually to find that the plane is half empty.

A jumble of noise came out of the speaker and several of us leapt towards the check-in counter. First to reach it was an elegantly attired Australian professor. Check-in was quite orderly and it appeared there would be enough seats for the half dozen passengers.

As the only two Europeans, the doctor and I were soon hunched over tepid coffee with a mud bank of sweet, glutinous sugared milk lining the bottom of the cups. He seemed to find the whole scene very amusing, and it made me realise that I had spent enough time in the country to miss the incidents and objects that instantly struck newcomers as remarkable.

Tom Stapleton was the name of my new companion and his reason for going to Bario was connected with one of Sarawak's well known figures, Tom Harrisson. After the Second World War, Harrisson started to work for the Sarawak museum, and with his specialised knowledge he acquired many native relics, including some unusual Chinese jars. In recognition of the co-operation and generosity of the Kelabit penghulu and his family, and through a fund set up for military service rendered during the war, Harrisson undertook to arrange for a Western education for the penghulu's grandson. The plan worked well and after studying in Australia the grandson, Dom Matou, qualified as a doctor and returned to Sarawak. Tom Stapleton had been the examiner for some of Dom Matou's final examinations and had got to know him well. Now he had come to visit Dom Matou's family.

We soon found ourselves flying over the unending sameness of the tropical jungle. Silver ribbons of river wound their way gracefully across the green blanket of trees. It is always interesting to fly over an area where one has either travelled by land or river. Instantly one can see the quickest and the easiest route. The two are very rarely the same. The Baram winding up to Marudi progresses through some enormous loops, yet when on the river one seems only to make a few turns in an otherwise fairly straight course.

The valleys and hills that mark the approach to the Kelabit Highlands suddenly present themselves in the distance like Plasticine on a model relief map. The closer we approached the easier it was to see how difficult the terrain would be for people on foot. To advance a short horizontal distance it would be necessary to go up and down an endless succession of steep hills. In the end one would have covered much more ground climbing and descending than advancing forwards. Detours around steep hills are exhausting because of the angled path; here one would always be leaning to one side to preserve balance. The plain of Bah where Bario is located appears quite suddenly out of the profusion of hills. It is like a lost city and indeed for years it was. Tom Harrisson's book on Bario, *World Within*, best describes the isolated yet prosperous community that lies on this large, fertile plain surrounded on all sides by ranges of mountains. There can be few places in the world that have absorbed the best of modern ways and rejected the worst. Bario and the whole Kelabit Highlands is one of them. It is approachable only by aircraft, or a tiring two-week long river and walking trip from the coast.

There are no cars and buffalo provide the only means of power transport. The climate at over three thousand feet is a pleasing warmth in the day and coolness at night. The stifling humidity that plagues the coastal areas is just a dim recollection and it is an excellent demonstration of how varied the interior of Borneo can be. The thick clayey soil washed from the surrounding hills produces excellent crops year after year so the best tag to find on a bag of rice says 'Bario Rice', although the finest comes from slightly further south.

Most of the central plain is under a complicated system of wet padi cultivation and on the small grassy knolls dotted around the plain stand the longhouses and individual dwellings of the Kelabit people.

The penghulu was at the airport to meet the plane as he is responsible, in conjunction with the border scouts, for checking passes. (It is still necessary for any non-Kelabit, including other

natives, to obtain a pass to go to Bario. This stems from an old Rajah Brooke ruling made to prevent Ibans and others from inter-tribal warfare.) This was Penghulu Ngimat Ayu, successor to the penghulu who had been Harrisson's colleaque. He asked Tom Stapleton and me to wait at the airport while he organised the slaughtering of a buffalo that was to be flown to Miri.

We decided to watch. The assigned beast was on its side with its head tied back, the chief executioner was to be the Muslim medical dresser. Bario is a Christian area but the meat was destined for Muslim consumption in Miri so it had to be slaughtered according to Islamic law. Work could not begin until it was certain the plane would land.

When the animal was in pieces and on its way to Miri, we were assigned a helper with a wheelbarrow to trolley our bags to where we were staying. It turned out to be a single house set on a low hill complete with two brass Chinese cannons guarding the approach.

The penghulu's step-son was living there with his wife who was Dom Matou's sister; thus was a link established between the old and the new rulers.

The house had many modern conveniences but the cooking was done by an Indonesian girl on an open fire in a back room. It was a remarkably efficient method. The amount of wood needed to produce the necessary heat was carefully controlled by the angle at which the individual faggots were placed. Smoke was minimal because of the dryness of the wood and also the type they were using. Firewood was stored directly overhead which helped to dry it out and in the cool evenings everybody sat around the fire and warmed themselves.

Regular flights to and from Miri to pick up surplus rice and buffalo meat meant that many modern conveniences and comforts could be brought into Bario homes without upsetting the balance of their general way of life. The inaccessibility of getting there in the past had saved them from headhunting Ibans, and now it was saving them from the more doubtful advantages that people of the civilised world have come to depend on.

It is ironic that such a secluded spot should twice in recent times have been the centre of military activity: first, towards the end of the last war when Allied parachutists, including Harrisson, descended on the unsuspecting populace to organise a revolt against the Japanses from the interior; and secondly in 1963 when Indonesia attempted to overrun Sarawak, and British and Gurkha troops used Bario as one of their front line bases. It would seem that the Kelabits have gained from these two experiences, from the building and

Evening, and farmers lead their buffaloes back to their Bario long-houses. Inset, Tom Stapleton and Kelabit friend.

hardware that the troops left behind and from the interest subsequently taken in the welfare of the Kelabits by people lilke Harrisson, whose name will be always linked with this area. Another indelible name is that of Mr Hudson Southwell of Marudi, who pioneered Christianity there. He told me how a boat of Muruts and Kelabits arrived in the 1930s and asked him specifically to come up and spread his teaching to them. As he was having an unresponsive time with the Ibans he agreed to go.

Through the help of a Kelabit in Miri, I was programmed to

follow what sounded an exciting route to a cave full of skulls where the Kelabits hid the heads of deceased citizens to prevent enterprising Ibans from digging up a skull, and running back home with a 'kill'; then on to some stones covered in ancient carvings; and finally to the site of an abandoned longhouse which apparently the Kelabits had searched for for years without success until 1974, when a group of hunters rediscovered it.

Instructions completed, my guide briefed, we set off for the skull caves of Buduk Batuh near the longhouse at Pa'Derong. We hacked our way through a marshy bit of jungle and came across some small caves recessed in the ground; my heart beating, my camera cocked I peered in to see the macabre scene. Nothing, absolutely nothing.

'Where are the skulls?' I asked.

'Throw away already . . . Christian no good.'

'Throw away where?'

'Throw into river; but Tom Harrisson takes some first for museum in Kuching.'

It was difficult to hide my disappointment and I took a picture of him instead. I started to stalk out of the marsh when he called back and as a consolation prize showed me a broken jar that 'had contained a body until recently'.

We had some tea in Pa'Derong longhouse and I then drummed him up to go to the carved stones. We walked through much lighter forest. Rhododendrons and delicate higher altitude flowers were blooming all around. The sun was hot, but it was not humid and in the shady paths with the profusion of flowers and carpets of pitcher plants I found walking most enjoyable.

Everything that is pleasant on the lowlands is doubly attractive higher up. The hot sun is pleasantly warm, the air is dry instead of damp, the tangle of plants gives way to a more delicate and numerous flora, while the rivers are shallow, clean, pebbly and easily accessible.

The guide had been used regularly by Harrisson and was very well trained in naming anything of the slightest interest without having to be asked.

We reached Pa'Ara at midday. There were plenty of large stones around, and my guide took me to where there was an indentation in the ground and looked solemnly at it.

'They can't have thrown away a two ton rock. Where is it?' I asked.

'Take away already.'

'Who take away?'

'Tom Harrisson, for museum in Kuching,' and to emphasise his point he insisted on showing me where Harrisson had camped during the stone removal operations.

'Well, I think we better get something straight now, has he been tampering with the abandoned longhouse?'

'No, he couldn't find it.'

'Phew, let's go.'

At three o'clock we passed a little shelter and he started dawdling and finally suggested we stayed there the night, but my blood was up and I insisted on pushing on.

By five thirty, my pack was getting heavy, and the football boots that had replaced my jungle boots had rubbed a couple of juicy blisters on my heels; I began to wish I had taken his advice and stopped at three o'clock. Finally as it was getting dark I limped into our destination at Pa'Bayoh. It was fairly dark so I did not register any surprise at not being able to see anything. We patched up a small shelter used by hunting parties and cooked up our food. I cracked open the whisky and crouched in our little shelter with the sound of buzzing insects and listened to his war stories against the Indonesians in 1963.

It poured with rain most of the night, and at the screech of dawn the leeches struck. As soon as it was light enough he took me to the longhouse location. I expected to see some old timbers and at least a small sight of debris from a former longhouse, but there was nothing. He kept pointing in an imaginary line to show where the longhouse stood, but I was still unable to convince myself that I could see anything. One thing did stand out and that was the excellent location, set near the wide curve of the Bayoh river. This is one of the small rivers that empty into the source of the Baram. A small clearing on the far bank due to pig rootling activity let in a patch of sunlight that illuminated this tranquil spot.

The last piece of evidence he showed me before we set off back was a stone shelter set in the bank. Undoubtedly man-made, it seemed just as likely to have been a temporary shelter as part of a longhouse complex.

After perusing this final fiasco for a few minutes and taking another photograph of my guide, we headed back. We followed an unused path that had overgrown with the shark-toothed vine. It caught in our clothes and skin every few minutes; bands of monkeys called out their 'Wa wa wa' noise and went swinging away in a flurry of shaking branches when they caught sight of us. Birds kept up an orchestra of sounds all around and an occasional pig would make noises. Whenever this happened my guide would pluck a sliver of leaf, place it between his two thumbs and blow through them to make a rasping noise that was supposed to attract them. After a few puffs he would go slinking off with his gun to where he thought the pig was. Half an hour later he would return with a 'no good' gesture. Time and again this hopeless ritual was followed, and I decided that my next guide would not be allowed a gun.

Back at Bario, Tom Stapleton told me he had visited some of the nearby longhouses and done a 'spleen count' on the children. This apparently is a quick way of determining whether a child has had malaria. If his spleen feels enlarged then he has had an attack.

In the Bario area the incidence of malaria is fairly low but further away in the Kelabit Highlands the Penans, especially at Pa'Tik, had been suffering from a virulent strain of chloroquine resistant malaria that had killed twenty-eight Penans in the last few months, and was continuing with its deadly toll. In former days when an infectious disease struck a village the inhabitants would distribute themselves into the jungle until the scourge died out. Now they wait patiently and fatally for somebody to bring the white man's medicine.

Tom was very amused at my failed trip and was all for going off to 'really find the skulls', but he could not get a volunteer to take him. He was even more put out when they went off hunting with a pack of dogs and left him behind. I tried to explain that as his only footwear was a pair of slippery-soled city brogues they may have left him behind for his own benefit. 'Nonsense. I can walk and run all day,' he said.

The clouded leopard is one of the most impressive animals in the Bornean jungle, and unfortunately it now seems to be fairly rare. However, hanging in the main room where we were staying was a magnificent skin, killed two months previously at Pa'Main. Killing a leopard apparently is not as dangerous as one would imagine. Once it is cornered it more or less gives up and makes it easy for the man to get close and spear it. This is usually done in the top of the tree. I would not like to put this to the test but the increase in the number of guns means this beautiful creature has a very bleak future ahead, and even national parks, such as that at Gunung Mulu, are quite powerless to operate an effective policing of the area.

Before crossing the border I was anxious to make a southern circuit of the Kelabit Highlands on foot. The old guide had had enough, so engaging a new one, this time without a gun, we set off to the salt springs at Pa'Main, intending to be away from Bario for about a week.

Salt is the great trading commodity that coastal traders use when they barter for native goods. However in the highland areas there are many places where the springs are brine instead of fresh water, and from these they process enough salt for their requirements.

We walked along well cleared paths for several hours and arrived at a very neat compound producing blocks of salt by boiling away the water. A small catchment area had been constructed where the water bubbled out. In a shed beside this catchment area were half a dozen fires evaporating the water and leaving blocks of rather grey salt that has a slight taste of iodine as well. These salt springs have a dual function; in dry weather animals congregate around them, presenting an easy target for the native hunters.

From the salt springs we visited the old longhouses and farmhouses at Pa'Main. During confrontation with Indonesia the people were moved from this area. It is also the most ancient record the Kelabits have of their origin. Before Pa'Main they can only speculate where they were.

From Pa'Main we continued south on a little used track. We passed a group of trees that the honey bears had been using for toning up their claw muscles. Seeing the lacerations in the tree trunks I was most anxious we would not come face to face with one of these beasts on the track. It is quite a common form of accident for a native to come face to face with a bear on a path and for the animal to attack instead of running away.

Again and again we had to cross over gullies and swiftly flowing streams. This highland area is pitted with these natural hazards as soon as one leaves the main path. The studs on my football boots were very unsuitable for traversing some of the slippery logs, often no more than four or five inches wide and rounded on the walking surface. Practice helped and I developed a technique of turning my feet inwards so that the smooth surface between the front and back studs took my weight.

Long Dano is another clean, well located longhouse, but unfortunately the population was dwindling rapidly. Most of the young men had hived off to the imaginary greener grass near the coast, which had created a severe manpower vacuum. The headman was also the deputy penghulu of the Kelabits and was bemoaning how he was ever going to be able to build a landing strip for the small mission plane or have enough strong hands to ensure the survival of his longhouse. He again brought up the rumour that one hears wherever one travels in the interior: 'The English promised to come back if we needed them. We need their help now.'

Even allowing for a natural tendency to complain, this particular sentiment is so widespread that I later discovered its origins lay in the two transfers of power: first when the British took over from the Brookes and second when Malaysia took over from Britain. In both cases the agents appointed to explain and advise the natives on which way to vote used the conciliatory argument that if things went wrong under the new order, the English would come and help them. This of course they did when Indonesia attempted to invade in 1963, but it was never intended to mean that a direct form of rule would ever again be envisaged. Possibly the headman was just old fashioned; he still flew Rajah Brooke's flag in his longhouse.

Under Malaysia the natives have had an enormous increase in living standards and many new opportunities have been opened to

More wrist watches than 'long ears' — highland chiefs meeting in Bario show many signs of change.

them, but what they think they remember enjoying was the old system whereby a white district officer actually made regular visits to the longhouses and after settling any problems more or less left them to order their own lives.

As an example of people living well ordered, well balanced lives, treating nature with respect and not abusing their natural resources, the Kelabits have a lot to teach Western community planners.

The headman asked me how he should try to save his longhouse. I told him that just as his young men headed for a different environment in the towns , so were there hordes of city-encapsulated people in places like London who would be delighted to be issued with free land to farm, and such a pleasant place to live.

'Would they come if I asked them?'

'I'm sure they would, but your government wouldn't allow it.'

He brushed that aside and called a meeting of elders to discuss an influx of 'Buda Matas' (white eyes). Included in the meeting were a selection of girls who were consulted on their feelings about having European husbands. Everybody agreed it was a good idea, and before I departed he again reiterated his desire to put this plan into action.

Close to Long Dano was the superbly located complex at Pa'Dalih. Coming over the hill I found the small village nestling in a small protective plain with a delightfully meandering river flowing along one edge. The forest-clad hills were all around, some with light green patches indicating the cultivation of padi, but mostly the fertile soil on the plain produces crop after crop of the best quality rice. The sun was shining brightly in a cloudless sky as we walked down to the buildings. A few buffalo were grazing, and as I walked past the school the teacher came out to greet me; leaving his class unattended, he walked to the first longhouse to introduce me to the family of a Kelabit friend of mine in Miri.

The greeting was typically friendly, and bowls of fruit, such as papaya, mango and jackfruit were put in front of me, while they quickly killed a chicken and cooked it in a tasty, if rather hot sauce. Whenever I left a Kelabit longhouse they would offer me a parcel of food for my journey. Inside the banana leaves would be fruit, rice and salted fish. The fish were trapped in wicker baskets submerged in the padi fields.

A brisk walk for three hours brought us to Rumudu, a large flourishing community. The longhouse was two enormous parallel barracks with connecting passages every fifteen yards. The total length was about a hundred yards. All down the huge room were individual little fires around which different families were seated. Places round the fire are reserved for the older people to sleep. The height of the room was about twenty-five feet and the width about thirty feet. The timbers for the structural beams and floorboards are of huge dimensions, some floorboards being three to four feet wide.

Rumudu had a very stony river which was difficult to cross, its banks consisting of large rocks covered in sharp slivers of shale. The headman was away, and his two plump, friendly daughters took over responsibility for my arrival. By now my feet and ankles were extremely painful so it was a great joy to be received where there was no feeling of pressure or imposition, and people pursued questions just as long as one seemed happy to answer them.

My football boots were causing me such pain that I was on the point of discarding them, but this would have been worse; without the toughened soles from years of going barefoot, one would not have lasted half an hour over the uneven surface.

My guide was also complaining of aching feet, so we made a promising couple hobbling along the paths and over the rickety rotan bridges. Near the longhouses the rivers are crossed with the aid of split bamboos placed end to end, supported on a network of rotan creepers. Some of these perilous looking constructions are as much as sixty or seventy feet long, and they sway and creak with one's weight.

At one point in the path I heard a cracking of branches and a large monkey came flying down from about hundred feet up; he broke his fall once at about forty feet on a dead branch, and after landing on the ground close to where I was, bounded away. For a moment I thought it was out of control and about to attack, but my guide explained that it was normal for this type of monkey to make for the ground before making good its escape.

Twice we passed Penans out with their blowpipes, and trying out my 'Koko ma ka tie?' was pleasantly surprised when they answered with the equivalent of 'for a little walk'.

We continued our own long walk for five hours, and suddenly, after being in primary jungle all the way, came out into a small clearing where there was a house, a fence, a dog, a pig and a little stream.

It seemed utterly out of context, like the gingerbread house fairy tale.

We stepped up to the door and rapped on it; slowly it opened to reveal a charming young woman; the illusion was complete. She spoke in good English, asking us where we had come from. Her parents were away, but she prepared some boiled pig for us, with bananas and rice, and pressed us to stay for the night. It was a tempting offer, and my guide firmly declared that he was going to do just that. As it was only midday I wanted to push on a bit further and suggested he catch me up later; this galvanised him into action and with our benefactor urging us not to go, we perversely hobbled off into the gloomy arms of the forest. The girl had explained to me that they were moving from Rumudu to Bario, and had built this farm as a staging post for moving their belongings.

Another half hour's walk and we came upon a small Penan settlement, Pa'Beraan. The shacks were in poor shape, each one big enough for about six people. There were no men around at all, just a few children and women, all of them drained and weakened by malaria. These were not the robust type of Penan from the Linau, and I imagine that it was the bad outbreak of malaria that was partially responsible.

The government had been following a regular policy of spraying all areas around longhouses with D.D.T., but in Bario, they had told me that recently this policy had lapsed. It would probably be better it they had never started it in the first place as the mosquitoes had returned tougher, stronger and more aggressive than ever before.

At long last we were back again in Bario but by now my legs had practically gone numb. Tony's wife, Marilyn, told her Indonesian helper to fetch Micky, a Murut, who was a celebrated masseur. Micky the Murut arrived and gently kneaded my knotted thigh and calf muscles. I wasn't expecting it to do much good, but surprisingly his adroit fingers loosened the muscles and eased the aching, so that I was able to get a good rest.

The guide who had accompanied me had previously volunteered to show me the way across the border but he suddenly disappeared and I never saw him again. The walk should not have been tiring for him; it is an indication of the easier life they have now.

The penghulu at Bario came over the next day to hear a debrief of my walk. He first of all asked me, 'Did the guide take you to some carved stones?'

'No, but he did point vaguely into the distance and mention something about rocks, and when I suggested going he said it was difficult.'

'I told him to take you to some ancient carved rocks. Do you want to go and see some at . . .'

I looked at the two holes in the back of my heels, took a sip of whisky, half closed my eyes and conjured up a painted cave of multicoloured dancing figures and decided to leave the whole thing in the realms of fantasy.

'No. Thank you for offering, I'll try them another time.'

The penghulu stayed well into the evening discussing his work as leader of his people and the direction he hoped they were going in the future. Perhaps it was more difficult and frustrating to live here than it appeared. One thing was certain; under his benevolent and wise counsel the people could not hope for a better advocate for their grievances.

After two days' rest, and having fortunately found a pair of jungle shoes of a more flexible nature than my football boots, I was ready to set out for Kalimantan. I walked to the nearby longhouse at Pa'Ukat, as the first stage of the journey, where a naming ceremony was taking place in the evening. Custom dictates that parents and grand-parents also change their name, so they become 'mother of Johnny' or 'grandmother of Johnny'. Under the dictates of the B.E.M., the feast consisted of hot sweet powdered milk, cough sweets, rusks, pork and mashed rice. Over eight hundred people came, and looking around the sea of faces, all adorned in their traditional clothes and decorations, I imagined what noise and confusion there would have been if they had been allowed to drink. Everybody was grouped in the big public gallery of the longhouse, and there was a delayed reaction to the central proceedings. The

A Kelabit woman wraps cooked rice in leaves — a convenient lunch for a jungle traveller.

people near the couple would be bowing their heads while the people seventy yards further down would be laughing at a joke made a minute previously.

The day I wanted to cross the border happened to be a Sunday and in order for somebody to break the no work rule an exceptionally high price was being asked as guide fees. I considered it for a while and after deciding that it was bad policy to give way to inflationary wage demands, had the general direction pointed out, and then trusting more to luck than my compass I set off on my own.

Following a compass bearing is very difficult because of the necessity to follow contours. One can often be walking in the wrong direction to get on to an easier stretch of terrain in the right direction.

In addition, being hemmed in by the trees and foliage makes it impossible to take regular bearings from high ground. The natives always mark their route, in case they get lost or injured, by making a cut in various trees that they pass. Often they adopt a more complicated system of showing where they passed. A stick has some shavings made on it to show how many people went by and a leaf will be impaled on top to show that there is food in the area.

I took some dried fish and rice wrapped up in banana leaves and started following the track that I hoped would lead me to Kalimantan. The track often came to a fork, or had other tracks leading off; these were either game tracks or hunting paths, but following the instructions from the headman I made my way up two steep hills. My aneroid measured them at three thousand, six hundred and fifty feet and three thousand, seven hundred and fifty feet respectively. At some point I must have crossed the border; perhaps at a small, bubbling river between these hills. On top of the second hill was a fire clearing of about an acre, giving a magnificent view all around.

Walking alone through the jungle heightened my senses. I seemed to notice more plants and animals, twice I saw a big rusa cross the path ahead of me. I could walk at exactly my own pace, stopping to look at some giant insect or rest by a small stream and contemplate the unceasing activity that characterises the insect life on the ground and on the trunks of the trees. With no guide anxious to reach a longhouse before nightfall, without the unease created by his mere presence I could absorb and observe the jungle at leisure. The only distraction was a constant niggling concern that until I reached my destination I could always be going the wrong way. It did not matter how often I seemed to pass some landmark that tallied with the directions I had been given, I never felt entirely sure until I first sighted the cleared jungle that heralded padi fields and people.

I even felt an inverted sense of elation from the element of danger. I sometimes half hoped I would find myself lost so that I could see whether I would manage to select the right plants, roots and fruits to eat. I felt a great desire to test my ability to survive in a place where I knew it was possible, but difficult; but then again the better I was prepared, the less likely it was that these interesting lessons could ever be learnt.

9

Into Kalimantan

The final descent to Pa'Butul in Kalimantan was marked by a magnificent glimpse of jungle-clad hills and sweeping cultivated plain. One moment I was walking doggedly along, the next I was faced by this vision of safety. It came so suddenly that I stood and admired the panorama for several minutes. The corrugated iron roof of the border police building glinted brightly across the treetops. Walking along further, I was descending through damp jungle. When I had been high up, the sun had been able to penetrate so that there were dry banks of grass and brightly coloured rhododendron flowers giving the scene an added touch of interest, but once back under the canopy, it was a return to the litter of rotting wood and leaves, the looping leeches streaking towards the warmth of a body, the slimy slippery rocks jutting from beneath the surface or providing hazardous stepping stones across a bubbling stream swollen by rain in the night. Occasionally a damp marshy patch with a trickle of water leading down a clearly defined route showed that rivers had to start somewhere. The rocky nature of the hillside created silvery waterfalls and crystal clear pools where minute fish swam. Sometimes a gully would have a series of falls, pools and overhanging rocks creating natural grottoes. Few beverages taste as exquisite on a parched throat as the clear, sweet water from these rocky pools.

At the bottom of the hill was a buffalo swamp, and it was impossible to circumnavigate it. Having meticulously kept myself out of the mud on my walk, I was now knee deep in stinking buffalo mire. The border guards were asleep so I strolled through the kampong. Children ran about excitedly announcing the unusual sight of a European emerging from the jungle without a guide. It was a village of Muruts and presently after a wash in the stream I was comfortably installed in a longhouse. As in Bario the fireplaces were prominently placed although they were open only on three sides. The altitude was about two thousand eight hundred feet, making it quite chilly at night.

Communication had been getting easier as constant practice with the aid of my phrasebook had enabled me to conduct simple conversations. I was no longer at a loss to explain where I had come from, where I was going, what I was doing and so on. Fortunately Indonesian is very close to Malaysian, and a Malaysian expression is instantly understood in Kalimantan.

There was no problem following the wide plain along to Long Bawan. As I walked I would be joined at different stages by inquisitive people, who would insist when we passed their house or their friends' houses that I have some food; even limiting myself to a single banana or small fish, by the time I reached Long Bawan I was feeling very full indeed. I approached Long Bawan with some trepidation as there was no official immigration office here for non-natives, and having heard on the Malaysian side about the arbitrary manner in which the Indonesian police can act, I was hoping that I would not be arrested on suspicion, pending further enquiries.

Very great was my surprise, therefore, when an official in the district office was extremely friendly, instantly inviting me to stay with his family, and insisted on accompanying me to see the police to help with formalities. In the police camp I was treated with the same friendliness. They were more interested to know about my walk and what things cost in Bario than in applying the third degree. Even when forms had been filled in and details given the gratuity payment requested was so small I nearly paid it, but having paid for a visa in Kota Kinabalu I merely said I had already paid enough, and they were not in the least put out. He shook my hand and wished me a pleasant stay in Indonesia. This of course was not the end of the story. I still had to enter the country officially and this necessitated what would almost certainly be a sticky interview in Tarakan, on the coast.

The official I was staying with took me back to his house and had his wife prepare a banquet of chicken, fish, buffalo, various vegetables and fruit.

I told him of my plans to walk to Malinau from Long Bawan and catch a boat from there.

'You must see the camat (district officer). He knows the route to follow.'

So later in the day when the camat had returned to his office, I was extended treatment that was the complete antithesis of Sar-

Musical instruments are often homemade. These Kelabit children entertain visitors to Bario.

awakian officialdom.

'You want to walk to Malinau? Well, you know the mission plane goes regularly, and as nobody walks any more the paths are overgrown, but if you really want to go, this is the best way . . . '

Whereupon he pulled out maps, showed me the route and then wrote down the names of the villages and approximate walking times between each. 'You'll need a guide,' and shouting for a junior told him, 'Get me a man who is available to start walking now.' I was completely overwhelmed; the difference between a co-operative official and having to avoid them was quite stunning. I even felt I was being organised to do something I did not really want to do. I had only just arrived and was very tired. Short rations, blistered feet and the beginnings of a light fever did not seem the most promising start to a very long, hard trip. I am quite certain if I had had to search round the village for a reluctant guide and been forced to frog-march him through the jungle I would have gone, but with a guide sprucely turned out, raring to go, I was the reluctant party. I thanked the camat profusely, used my guide as far as the house I was staying in, and sent him back to his hut.

The camat's plan was a series of instructions in the following vein: 'Pa'Milan-Long Serabin thirty hours (actual walking time), three mountains, two to three nights in the jungle.' What finally decided me against this route was that there seemed to be little of interest on the way. The villages I would have passed through were very poor Murut communities, who would have been engaged in harvesting at the time. I wanted to get to the Kayan Hilir and Kayan Hulu and there seemed little point in walking across the Krayan division.

The next two days were enlivened by large quantities of Chinese brandy and the antics of a Murut teacher. Chinese brandy tastes like the home distilled liquor in the Middle East called 'flash', and it has something added to give it a brownish colour. The Murut teacher came from Sarawak, spoke excellent English and contained more nervous energy than anybody I had ever met. He had set himself the task of teaching everybody in Long Bawan English, and his voluntary classes were very well attended from the D.O. downwards. I later discovered that all the English spoken by the officials I met was solely the result of this man's efforts. He had even started teaching English to the children in the school although this was not on their syllabus.

Long after I had gone to bed and midnight had past I could hear the Murut teacher with another batch of adult pupils: 'This is *his* hand, this is *his* foot, this *her* nipple.' Many of them had only learnt parrot-like statements and after shaking your hand with 'Good day, sir, and how are you? It's good to have you here,' would be unable to speak another word. I learned to distinguish between the non-speakers and the ones with limited knowledge. The more confidently they announced their greeting the less likely they were to be able to follow it up.

Drinking in the official's house continued into the day; their capacity for consuming alcohol was remarkable. Skinny fellows weighing about a hundred pounds poured enormous quantities of alcohol into themselves and remained the epitome of affability. While we drank and communicated in pidgin Indonesian, Malaysian and English, a native with a head-covering resembling a woollen tea cosy knocked at the door. He wanted an identity card photograph, so my host pulled out a tripod and an ancient camera from beneath a piece of furniture and started to set it up. His social obligations had reduced him to a state that made this operation difficult. His attempt at adjusting the tripod to suit the level of the subject was frustrated by the legs continually falling off. If I had not been concentrating on controlling my laughter I would have shown him that he was already at maximum elevation. Finally he seemed fully set, disappeared under a black cloth and for a long time remained static. Then pulling away the cloth, he decided to raise his subject and children were sent to collect pieces of wood to place under the placid native. When the native was eventually perched on a pile of firewood with his legs dangling, his tea cosy was removed, a couple of chickens which had come in with the firewood were chased squawking from the room and the picture was taken. The click of the camera was a cue for everybody to give vent to their emotions, and an uproarious scene followed with everybody congratulating the beaming official on his photographic prowess, and hooting with laughter. The official sat down with a broad grin; he had just completed his day's work.

The teacher then started a dissertation on what he had done for Long Bawan. I happened to comment in the middle of his tirade on what a pleasant change it was to see girls in hot pants instead of sarongs. 'I did that, I did that.' He jumped from his chair in a frenzy of emotion, '*I put them into hot pants.*'

'Bravo!' We all clapped and cheered him, while he sank back into his seat, aware that he had gone slightly out of control.

Whenever he was around I never had a dull moment. His family was in Lawas in Sarawak, but he did not intend going back to them unless it was at the head of a revolution. 'I fought for Malaysia in the 1963 confrontation, but I'd never do it again; the only thing now that the government takes an interest in, is trying to convert us to Islam. This doesn't happen in Indonesia. Indonesia is much better!'

The morning that the mission plane was due, I walked the twenty minutes to the strip. Schoolchildren were cutting the grass on the runway by hand. As the plane approached they all scattered into the bush. In addition to the mission plane, Bali Air and Bouraq (nothing to do with the drink) also had scheduled services into Long Bawan.

'Chuck' Smith was the pilot, and he bore the countenance of long sufferance. Day after day for a very small salary he flew people and supplies around the small jungle strips, sometimes doing as many as twenty landings in a day when people needed shuttling over a short distance. His organisation was M.A.F., the Mission Aviation Fellowship. The contribution from these planes to native life is enormous. A coastal trip is now a matter of hours instead of months, but it also means that all the old paths and routes are being forgotten through lack of use. Furthermore if a native cannot afford to pay the plane fare it is extremely difficult for him to find a group of people whom he can join for a trip down to the coast.

The missionary pilots do all their own maintenance, and arrange for strips to be made in new areas.

Chuck (what else could a bush pilot be called?) flew me down to Malinau in the morning and said he could pick me up in the afternoon to go to Tarakan. Flying over the hills east of Long Bawan I could see the jagged route I would have had to travel had I walked. I looked down at individual mountains and imagined how long it would have taken to cross them; I felt quite relieved that I was in the plane. Flying over the jungle gives one a better impression of where one is going when one does start to walk on a cross country route. As one traverses hills and follows small streams it is much easier to envisage the sense in it all, having seen it from above.

Malinau is about ninety miles from Tarakan up the Sesajap river, surrounded on all sides by nipah palm swamps. The river is about two hundred yards wide and the town is situated at the point where the river widens rapidly after its descent from the hills in the centre of the country.

Malinau is a fast-growing town, as many of the natives from the interior are moving here. Primarily it is Muslim, but there is a Roman Catholic Italian priest operating and an American missionary couple from the same organisation as M.A.F.

When we landed an American missionary woman appeared out of the bushes to see Chuck. She had pebble glasses and buck teeth. A dribbling child was being dandled in her arms. I asked her what church she represented; unfortunately I missed the complete name but it was something like, 'The Baptismal Episcopalian Church of Evangelism'.

'Is this the same as the Borneo Evangelical Mission?' I asked.

'Yeah, I guess it's pretty similar,' she said.

'How do you get on with the R.C.s and Muslims being in the town together?'

'We arranged to divide up the native population; it was quite amicable.'

Chuck flew off back to Long Bawan and I wandered around Malinau until the afternoon. Dirty coffee houses were full of dour looking people sipping thick coffee resembling drilling mud and nibbling on sweet cakes. It was with no regret that I made my way back to the strip and flew to Tarakan, an island off the east coast of Borneo.

After one drive through Tarakan I realised that this was a boom town, shoddily put together to cater for the exploitation of the oil and timber resources. Everything from banks to hotels looked as though it would blow away in a fair sized gale. The roads were appalling. Having once been sealed they were now worse from lack of maintenance than if they had been left as sandtracks. Innumerable potholes made it impossible for cars to avoid them. The ancient vehicles that ferried people around lurched from hole to hole with their occupants bouncing around inside like ice in a cocktail shaker. There were no buses, just the large Land-Rover and Toyota taxis which stopped without warning beside a flapping hand.

I had now crossed Borneo from west to east but not quite in the way I had intended. I had not meant to fly over so much of Kalimantan but had hoped to explore it in more detail. Somehow I must get back up into the hinterland again. Perhaps I could get a boat up one of the rivers; I thought I might go to Samarinda and start up the Mahakam river. So I went to enquire at a travel agent. Merpati planes were all broken down. Bali Air went only twice a week, and Bouraq was having one plane repaired while the other was booked ahead for the next two years.

I went back to my hotel, run by an enormous moustached fellow who kept waddling down the passage of his grimy inn, on to the verandah at the front where most of the guests sat staring blankly, belching very loudly and wandering back again into the dark recesses of some steaming ferret's nest that I could only imagine he slept in.

While engaged blankly staring with everybody else I noticed a native woman walk past with a Kenyah design on an article she was carrying. Accosting her, I tried to find out how she was going back to her longhouse, which must have been somewhere in the central plateau. Just as I was about to give up, one of the other guests intervened, and speaking adequate English explained that he was also Kenyah and would help me plan my route.

I was to get a boat to Tanjung Selor where he was a government official and get a pass to travel upriver. Once there he would go through with me all the places I should go to in order to reach Long Nawang. This had been my original destination before being so brusquely turned back by the police in Long Jawi. With this encouraging start I set off to see the immigration officer to give him the news of my arrival. Indonesians love uniforms, badges and generally behaving in a pseudo-military fashion. The immigration office was bristling with several grades of khaki, and a prominent notice warned visitors that 'incorrect dress or appearance is illegal'. A bedraggled line of illegal immigrants was lined up under the surveillance of an armed guard. I asked to see the chief officer and was ushered into a plush office with a lean, sinister-looking young man behind the desk. 'Yes?' he said abruptly.

'I've just entered the country through Long Bawan, I think I have to get an entry chop from here and not there.'

'You've done *what?*' He sprang up from behind his desk, knocking his pipe and ashtray on to the floor. 'This is strictly illegal.'

'Oh my God, I never realised. I told the Indonesian consulate in Kota Kinabalu that that was the way I was coming.'

'Did you?' He shot me a penetrating glance, wrenched the receiver off the ancient telephone and frantically wound the handle to call the operator. 'Hello, Central! Hello, Central!'

It sounded as though he was going to follow it up with 'Get me Doctor Jazz', but when the operator answered he told her to get Kota Kinabalu. He then called a junior and told him to get all the details from the consulate on my visa application. The junior disappeared to take over the call from a different line.

The end result was reasonably predictable. The junior returned some twenty minutes later with sheaves of information on everybody except me; after being screamed at that he was an imbecile he returned later with all information except where I had applied to enter from; more hysteria, and this time the chief gave me a slight raising of the eyes to show how difficult his job was. Minutes passed before a jittering junior returned to say that the line to Kota Kinabalu had broken down.

'Get out,' he roared at the junior and then to me, 'Give me your passport.' He opened it up at the page where the visa was and wrote down *Jalan kaki* (walked) and snapped a chop on to it. 'Enjoy your stay in Indonesia. Bali's better than Borneo, you know.'

'Oh is it? Thank you very much,' and I walked casually to the door, tipped myself out, and took off back to the obscurity of the inn.

By way of a diversion before catching my boat the following morning, I visited Tarakan's Disneyland called Kampong Gunung Lingkas. It only resembles America's Disneyland in the unreal world that faces one after paying to enter a village where all the activities of daily life are going on. There are shops selling everyday articles, coffee shops where one can sit and while away the hours. However the big difference is that the sixty females wandering around the place, washing their clothes, sitting and talking casually with one another or helping to serve in the shops, are all prostitutes. It is the essence of low pressure selling. The sixty Javanese girls came from Surabaya, and their range catered for every taste. They were friendly without being forceful.

It is quite in order to sit in the coffee houses without participating. Placed discreetly among the complex of constructions are several long, low buildings divided into cubicles. A central passage runs through the middle, and in taking a perambulation around the village all paths lead through at least one of these buildings, where girls who are bored with hanging around outside sit on their beds painting themselves or playing cards. Each girl is given one of these cubicles to use and decorate as she likes. There seemed to be very little activity there during the afternoon, and the number of girls heavily outnumbered the few skulking figures sniffing around. My guide assured me that at night time it was quite another scene. Above the entrance to this extraordinary complex was an official sign saying '*Wanita Semogasadar*' which is not a notably precise phrase but in its context means 'It is to be hoped that these girls know what they are doing (and will stop doing it)'.

Coastal towns around Borneo are hot and humid, and when it rains, mud and rubbish pour down the streets in waves of filth. They are the only places where Western-style platform shoes really come into their own. It is no surprise to see how popular they are in these places. It is unfortunate that Borneo is usually assessed on these coastal areas; a different world awaits those people who get into the highlands in the centre of the island.

After only a few days I was already feeling the urge to get away from the leeching climate of Tarakan; the environment of a Western-style city in this heat and humidity is particularly unpleasant. Tropical towns need to be built with open space and low buildings, but unfortunately air conditioning and economics are producing exactly the opposite.

Learning a smattering of Indonesian for communicating with the locals was not too difficult. With the Chinese I used English but the classic 'r' and 'l' interchange soon caught me out. I had sent a Chinese to get some medical supplies and was surprised to find an engineering lubricant among the goods he brought back.

'Which item is this?' I asked him.

He pointed at my list: 'Crotch cream for sweat rashes,' and said, 'I ask for clutch cleme and they send me to galage.'

I spent my last evening in Tarakan watching groups of Bugis labourers noisily playing pool in a saloon. They placed large bets on their own skill and with cigarettes clasped between their teeth, they strutted around the tables and jabbed at the balls with their cues, as if an aggressive approach would somehow help their game. Then, straightening up from the invariably inaccurate shot, they chalked their cues, blew a column of smoke and looked pained that they had failed to achieve what they had aimed for.

Rows of Javanese girls perched on high stools kept the scores on blackboards behind each table. Arguments broke out regularly, and a noisy exchange with the occasional scuffle would be followed by a disgruntled Bugis sloping off down the street.

A breakfast of red-hot curry set me on the road to the docks where a small boat ferried passengers to the express boat bound for Tanjung Selor.

10

Long Nawang

The sky was overcast and the mainland of Borneo was not visible from the boat. After half an hour the coast came in sight and gradually the swaying nipah palms standing with their bases submerged in the water came closer. We followed the coast for a short distance before turning up one of the narrow channels that wind in mazes through the swamps. When I had flown in I had entertained myself by fixing on a point in one of these channels and trying to follow a route that would lead to the large river. Sometimes I would trace miles of meandering waterways looping backwards and forwards on themselves, often coming within yards of river before the exit was reached. Skill and a good memory are needed to navigate these inlets.

Tanjung Selor is set a short distance up the Kayan river and is a Muslim enclave, as are all the river estuary towns. A ramshackle mosque and sultan's residence were visible on one bank while opposite stood the town. This is the administrative centre for the Kayan and Bahau river basins, two great rivers of northern Kalimantan. In the past it was the trading centre for native goods coming down from the interior.

It now had the usual complement of uniformed bureaucrats duplicating each other's work, but again I encountered helpful and obliging officers. This was almost certainly because they were natives and as such did not feel the need to keep me waiting to show how important they were.

My visit to the police with a request for papers to travel upriver was dealt with within two hours and a policeman was sent round to where I was staying with full documentation for my trip. Again it was a very different attitude from that of some Malaysian officials I

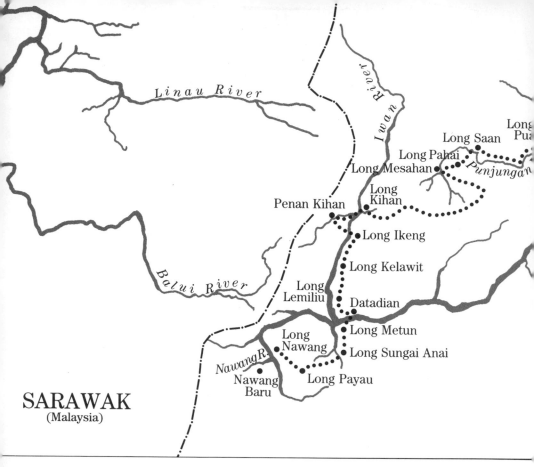

SARAWAK
(Malaysia)

had had to deal with.

The Kenyah gentleman who had been so helpful asked me to his house for dinner where a friend of his was going to help me plan an interesting route.

I arrived at his house and was treated with great hospitality. His friend turned out to be half Kenyah and half German, the son of a German doctor. His mixed parentage had given him a remarkably distinguished face. Fine featured, with deep-set grey eyes, his hair was brushed back and a smile continually placed about his lips. It gave him an aura of affluence and education. Only when he spoke to my friend in his native tongue and asked that I take down what he was going to tell me, because he could not write, did I see him as a local Bornean.

Decorating the walls of the house was a superb collection of native handicrafts, including a parang with every facet of the blade, handle and sheath worked with consummate skill. I commented on it, and my host told me that it had belonged to his father, a penghulu

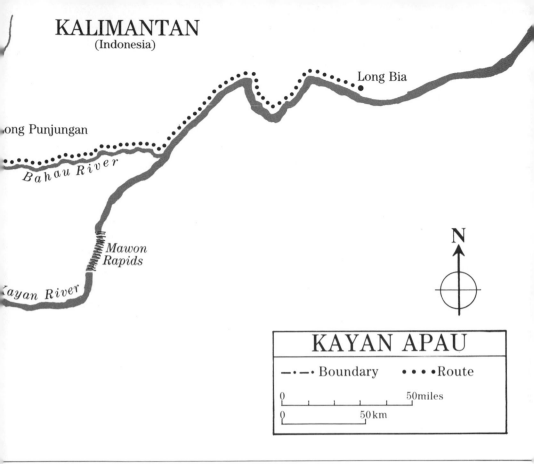

KALIMANTAN
(Indonesia)

Long Bia

ong Punjungan

Bahau River

Mawon Rapids

ayan River

N

KAYAN APAU
—·—· Boundary   • • •Route

0 _____ 50miles

0 _____ 50km

from Long Alang on the Bahau.

The next morning I agreed to meet him outside his office at eight o'clock to collect a map that he kindly said he would photocopy for me. At eight o'clock sharp I arrived at his office's location, which was part of complex containing all the civil service administration, records, files and papers for the whole area. The building occupied an entire block, or had done until three o'clock that morning. I met my friend but it was outside an acre of smouldering ruin. A few beams were still burning; about half a dozen boxes of files had been rescued from the whole building. A group of harassed officials were muttering more to themselves than to each other. Even with this shambles my friend managed a little humour. He greeted me with, 'I would have asked you in, but...' and he looked at the desolation. After a few words of empty commiseration I returned from whence I came, and set about finding a boat going upriver. As I walked back, the first helicopters started arriving with officers who would conduct the enquiry.

I soon discovered a small trading boat leaving at five o'clock the next morning for Long Bia, a day's trip upriver and I was pleased that a light fever which had been troubling me for three days reached its zenith during the evening, with rivers of sweat drenching my shirt. The Chinese boat driver had wanted so much to take me that I had not agreed, and just before the boat's departure I gave him a final offer of one-fifth the sum he had asked for. He accepted this figure grudgingly although it was double what he should have charged. Far up river where petrol is difficult to obtain a high price is reasonable but Tanjung Selor had every access to petrol from Tarakan and could not possible justify high transport charges.

We motored for nine hours up the Kayan river and must have covered about seventy miles before reaching Long Bia. On the way were innumerable kampongs of resettled natives. These people had moved either voluntarily or on government instructions to the easily accessible areas near the coast. Again in accordance with government policy, they had abandoned their longhouse system and lived in poky huts with a 'street' running between the two rows. I briefly visited three of these new villages and found them very depressing places; it was also noticeable that many more children had skin diseases in these places than I had seen before. In abandoning the airy, big proportions of the longhouses in favour of small, stuffy rooms, disease and germs had festered more successfully. Above all, the whole community feeling and attractions of the longhouse were lost where families kept to their own huts and rarely visited other ones. No more general work together on the common verandah where gossip and toil could be shared throughout the day. Sense of possession was much more marked in these huts, and I noticed that they had padlocks on the doors against intruders. In the journey up to Long Bia I counted ten villages, and they more or less alternated between Kayan and Kenyah. The overcrowding of kampongs in such a small area must lead to disputes over padi land, and the next step for these people is to join the Bugis and Bulungan in the pool halls and doss houses of Tarakan.

Long Bia is run by a Chinese patriarch married to a Kayan woman. His father had acquired the land, and he had offered a chunk of it to the K.I.N.G.M.I. (Gospel Tabernacle Christian Church of Indonesia) Church to start a mission school for training native pastors, and also to build an airstrip and hangar for the mission plane.

I was staying with this man who must have operated one of the remotest hotels anywhere. It chiefly caters for Philippines and Japanese timber company executives coming to recce the area. In accordance with native custom he did not charge me, because I was not there on business. I only met one of the missionaries on this occasion. He invited me round to his bungalow for dinner. It was run down, with the wooden chairs on the verandah broken and unpainted despite most of the materials being sent from America. We sat down carefully so as not to break the chairs further, and started talking about the missionary life. It is quite a safe topic because they usually like to talk about themselves, as well as expecting a certain amount of beligerence from people 'not in the profession'. As a guest I limited my questions to some of the more obvious points that people raise when they first think of missionary interference. He fielded everything with 'We don't do that,' or 'That's part of Christianity.' I left a more extensive discussion with him and the other missionaries until a later date. For three years he had lived on a remote river bank answering the call of God in teaching the heathen the path of Salvation, and it had obviously got him down. A native girl skipped past and deposited a banana skin under the verandah where we were talking. My host was up at the rail in a flash, roaring at her to come back and pick up the skin. He looked ready to commit murder as the little girl retrieved the skin, waltzed away and threw it under the next bungalow.

'Is it the climate?' I ventured, to offer an explanation for the vehemence of his reaction.

'No, no, they have to be taught.'

The patriarch's son who was planning a trip upriver was unable to go because the water was so low; in his opinion it would be at least another week before the river would be suitable again, so I too would have to change my plans.

Although the mission plane that was normally based at Long Bia was away being repaired, it seemed that Chuck was expected to fly in soon on his way to Long Nawang. I decided to try to get a lift from him if I could, rather than wait around for the river to rise.

Next day Chuck turned up. He said he was willing to take me so I clambered into the Cessna 180 and prepared myself to enjoy an aerial view of the jungle. Flying from lowland to highland is always interesting and this trip was no exception. The rivers could be seen to get narrower and faster flowing as the ridges of hills increased in height.

Long Nawang is set among a profusion of cultivated or formerly cultivated hills. I was surprised to see the extent of the farmlands, but as Long Nawang has been the Kenyah capital of Kayan Hulu for scores of years I should have expected it. As we circled the village complex, the full extent of this long-established centre could be appreciated. Built around two sharp curves of the Kayan river, it was

The penghulu of Long Nawang — a commanding voice and undoubted authority.

well protected by the rapidly flowing river on one side and steep hills on the other. The airstrip, which was very short, was constructed in 1974. It had been an immense task for it had meant moving a section of mountain with only the simplest of tools, local workers and native organisation but the M.A.F. had promised that they would use it if the people could built it. In viewing the hunk of hill that had been shifted it was extraordinary to think that they had used no mechanical aids at all, not even wheelbarrows. Before the construction of this strip and the introduction of outboard engines the travel time from the coast to Long Nawang had been three months. Unlikely as it may seem, this outpost had first been manned by a Dutch district officer in 1911. The Dutch government had been getting suspicious about Rajah Brooke's territorial expansion in Sarawak and consequently had sealed some colonial official's fate by making him represent their government in this remote spot.

Long Nawang is the most important Kenyah community. It is the oldest and for a long time had the largest population. The longhouses are of massive proportions in everything but length. Of the eight longhouses I do not think any exceeded about forty doors, but the height and breadth of the central area outside the headman's and penghulu's quarters were remarkable. The beams were of roughly hewn tree trunks and they must have taken scores of people to set them in position. The whole effect was one of light and air and cool space.

The penghulu was quietly chewing betel nut when I arrived, sitting surrounded by a few of the old men, no doubt discussing the harvest and other problems of the community. He received me very cordially and without any show of surprise. He called to his wife for a bottle of borak and we drained it off in the bottoms-up technique that seems to be the form. Tattooed on his arm was 'I am a Christian man', so no spirit appeasement was necessary.

The harvest was in full swing which meant that many of the people were staying on the farms. A huge Gawai feast was planned for late in the month when the harvest would be finished, but I realised that a Gawai at a Christian longhouse might be disappointing.

The penghulu was anxious to show me where sixty Europeans were massacred by the Japanese in the war. After the Japanese invasion of Sarawak the Europeans who were unable to escape made their way up to Long Nawang. The well documented story relates how a native porter with the Japanese group ran on ahead to warn the people in Long Nawang. The Dutch officers poo-pooed his story, saying the Japanese would never bother to come so far, and as a punishment for causing all the villagers to flee into the jungle they 'arrested' him.

The next morning it was all too true. The white flag decorated with a poached egg symbol came over the ridge, and without a shot being fired the Europeans were captured. Subsequently in several batches the problem of what to do with them was eliminated.

The patriarch in Long Bia had revealed a welcome cache of Scotch whisky. When he had displayed his store I had expected him to ask some fantastic price, but he did not do so and I bought some. In the evening in Long Nawang I offered the penghulu a bottle. He rapidly became very drunk, boasting about the peace he had brought to the region, how his influence had settled countless disputes, and what a tremendous role he was playing among his people. Although now an old man, he had a firm commanding voice and there was no doubting the authority he had. Perhaps anxious for him not to tarnish his image, his wife attempted to relieve him of his bottle, but he brushed her aside and continued to enjoy a break in what I imagine had been a long abstinence.

Under the Kenyah system of society the penghulu and his immediate family are not obliged to work in the fields. Instead each family contributes a little to his household, or works his farmlands for him. With this burden removed the penghulu could concentrate on being a gracious host; he talked endlessly about the history and

fables of Long Nawang and the immediate area, but unfortunately I was only able to get the gist of about half of it. Above everything he kept emphasising the stability he had brought to end disputes between his people, and how he had encouraged a new tolerance towards Ibans. Kenyahs traditionally hate Ibans, and they use the word Iban to refer to any enemy or undesirable. I asked a Kenyah why he disliked Ibans so much and he said 'Because they speak another language', but of course it lay in the repeated raids that headhunting bands of Ibans used to make on Kenyah villages. The most recent incidents were in 1963 when Iban scouts employed by the British army in Long Jawi and Long Busang exceeded their terms of reference and took heads from Javanese soldiers and Kenyah civilians. The penghulu described them as a huge number; but then to demonstrate the new accord he told me with pride that last year an Iban passing through the area had actually stayed in his longhouse.

We walked around the kampong together admiring the abundance of Kenyah architectural decorations on the small buildings previously used for festivals. Mausoleums are still covered with intricate designs and carved animals. One carved and painted animal was clearly a tiger and not a leopard; it was impossible to deduce where they had got the idea from.

Kenyah graves in this area are covered with intricate designs.

Several of the men wore barkcloth coats. Commissioning a tailor, I was briefly measured and work was started. Two days later my coat was ready but despite the measuring they had made it to the dimensions of a native and I could not get it on. Long Nawang must be one of the few places where the traditional crafts are still encouraged. Several huge drums ten feet long were hanging up and I saw a man at work on a new one. In each longhouse, a woman was weaving bead patterns on to the back of baby carriers and other articles. Goats were kept primarily to use their hair in decorating parangs and shields. Wood carvers were hard at work, and people talented at playing the sape and singing were left during the day to practise.

I walked to Nawang Baru, an even larger kampong than Long Nawang and on to another village about an hour further up the Nawang river. In both these places the longhouses had the same vast dimensions as at Long Nawang. Along the paths were fantastically carved and coloured totem poles marking grave sites.

With the disappearance of the European administrative officers and the general depopulation of the central areas, the younger people have much less contact with Europeans than their parents had, and outside the big villages of Long Nawang and Nawang Baru their image of white people is only what they have been told by their parents. Now that salt and sugar is flown up to jungle centres and distributed from them, very few people really need to make the trip to the coast.

Iban men, when they are young, usually go on a 'bejalai'. This is a Grand Tour where they are expected to acquire 'wealth' for their families and to gain experience of the world outside their longhouse, in order to give them some ability in dealing with their own problems and disputes. The system works well; but the Kenyahs and some other interior people do not have this pressure on them, and the men will spend all their lives in the same area following the same routine day after day. In the old days they had the occasional release of a headhunt or salt collecting trip to the coast. It is small wonder that now these two important distractions have been removed, they are moving away in droves, which the government encourages them to do. Missionaries have tried to introduce sports as substitutes for their old recreations, but with only partial success.

I declined the penghulu's kind offer of a boat ride to Datadian and set off on my own again to walk to Long Payau. I followed the Kayan river for a short distance and where it begins its one hundred and eighty degree loop I struck off east. Here the scenery changed from jungle paths to big rolling grassland hills, where the cut jungle, instead of reforesting itself, has become smothered in a thick choking grass.

In the afternoon I arrived at the small longhouse at Long Payau. It had a delightful stream that made washing and swimming a pleasure. I was also offered on arrival a bowl of honey and some melons. This was a delicious combination after a stiff walk. The profuse sweating and hard exercise in great heat bring on a craving for sugar and salt, which the natives spent so much of their time and effort procuring. Fresh honey is about the best way to satisfy this craving and the combination of sweetness with a newly plucked melon, still cool inside, was irresistible. There were so few people here that native pastors had not yet interfered and all their natural customs were in evidence. All the girls had cut ears with heavy weights and rings hanging from them. Little beaded caps were also worn, and their 'sarongs' were multicoloured aprons, open at the back or hitched to the top of their thighs. This of course showed off their tattoos, which the introduction of sarongs has eliminated.

On the verandah one man was busy boring a hole in a piece of metal with the aid of an instrument rather like a top which was made to revolve backwards and forwards by raising and lowering a circular piece of wood connected to the bore with strings. Great speed and friction could be effected from this device, and it was also used for making fire.

The evening was quiet; the headman's wife had a bad attack of fever and lay in front of the fire while her family sat around her. Oil was scarce so the only illumination came from the subdued flickering of the flames in the fire-place. I lay on the far side of the room and watched the headman quietly puffing his cheroot with one hand resting on his wife's shivering frame. Occasionally the fire would flare up a little and light his tired, resigned face, composed to any outcome.

The next morning I heard some people getting ready to go to Long Sungai Anai, so I joined their party. I preferred to find out where people were going first to see if it was approximately the way I wanted to go. I would then ask if I could accompany them. To do it the other way round usually meant that natives going to where I wanted to go anyway would pretend to be giving up time to act as guides just for me.

We walked all day crossing marshes on narrow, rotting bridging that sank into the soft ground as one walked over it. Sometimes it

Kelabit mother and child in Bario. How much of the old will have survived when this youngster grows up?

was hard to see where one submerged log carried on from the next. Farmhouses and padi storage huts were sometimes just visible in a cleared patch of hillside; at other times we passed quite close to them. Passing a fruit tree with large round fruits the size of oranges, I broke one open to discover luscious transparent flesh covering half inch long pips. Noting my enthusiasm, one of our company shinned up the tree and hacked down several branches covered with the fruit.

Long Sungai Anai was approached through a series of padi fields, some still being used, the others giving way to the coarse-bladed grass. There were four longhouses, again situated on a clean, fast flowing and accessible river. The headman was away, but his second in command took me to his quarters, and his womenfolk brought a selection of fruits. It was obviously some sort of fruit season although the month did not tally with what I had been told was the official fruit season for this area.

Long Sungai Anai had the feeling of a wealthy community; several modern appliances were around and the people were better dressed, and even had soap. Sometimes a headman or member of a longhouse will get a job in a timber camp or oil related survey near the coast, and seeing the need for more labourers will fetch a large number of people from his own longhouse. In a few months, with no overheads to pay, the natives will have saved enough to buy mirrors, scissors and sometimes ancient sewing machines. I noticed these objects were the first to arrive in a house that had earned some money. The most striking difference between the longhouses in Sarawak and Kalimantan was that the former invariably had at least one outboard engine belonging to the headman, while in the latter I came across none more than a hundred miles from the coast. The reason lay in the fact that when the river level was down, which it is much of the time, it is impossible to use outboard engines. Additionally, the cost of petrol — flying it one and a half hours from Tarakan — would be prohibitive.

Cassette recorders do not exist because battery supply is so difficult, and in Indonesia generally the natives are much poorer; or at least a far smaller proportion than in Malaysia have had the chance to earn money. Rich Sarawakian natives such as the Kelabits still use Indonesian natives as very cheap labour.

While I was eating the fruit, a native came and asked me to stay with his family. He wanted to learn some English and to tell me how he had once been to Singapore and peninsular Malaysia.

He told me he came from Long Bulan in Sarawak and had married a girl at Long Sungai Anai; hence his present residence. He suggested we go together to Long Metun where he was hoping to meet his sister who was returning from Datadian, and was later planning to go back to Long Bulun in Sarawak.

Together we made the walk to Long Metun. My pack, which weighed about fifty pounds and which had felt like a hundred pounds when I first started carrying it over the hills, was feeling lighter every day. My capacity for long stretches of walking was increasing, my feet were hardening up inside the fragile jungle shoes which I had stitched together with fishing line, and I was beginning to enjoy the physical process of the walk. No longer concentrating on keeping going I could observe the different plants and wildlife with more than just a passing interest.

Long Metun was large with six longhouses and about five hundred people. We spoke to the headman of the first longhouse and were escorted over the Metun river by means of one of the precarious rotan and bamboo suspension bridges which led to the chief's place.

As we approached a group of natives in the central area, I noticed what I immediately took to be a European hippie. He wore an Afrika corps cap and had hair, moustache and beard halfway down his chest. No native I have seen before or since had a beard or moustache or long straggling hair. Even after I was introduced to him and he just smiled, I assumed he was of European extraction, and tried talking to him in English. He gesticulated to show that he did not speak English and my friend told me that he was in fact the village headman. Sure enough he spoke to my friend, and asked us to his room. Inside, he asked to see my pass. I produced the piece of paper covered in official stamps and he studied it for a while, then asked someone to fetch some reading glasses. They were brought and he buried them among the wild strands of hair covering his face and re-examined the pass. When he was satisfied, he unrolled a stamp from a cloth, puffed on it a few times and carefully placed it on the paper. With great pressure he rocked the little stamp backwards and forwards on the form until a faint impression bearing the name of the village was imprinted.

As soon as this formality was completed he relaxed, and summoned the statutory fruit. Pineapple was included, and I can still remember that it was at the finest point of ripeness, and tasted exquisite.

Feeling more confident in Indonesian I endeavoured to compliment the chief on his head of hair; but inadvertently used *rumput* meaning grass instead of *rambut* meaning hair. Everybody collapsed with laughter, and the chief himself was shaking with such mirth that his roll of sugi, or chewing tobacco, popped out on to the floor. This roll of sugi was a special feature of his. According to how hard he was laughing his top lip would apply pressure to the compact lump and push it downwards. A light chuckle would scarcely make it visible but anything more intense and it would come rolling down, whereupon he would push it back up and try to control the extent of movement of his facial muscles. This made his shoulders shake violently.

Several men were wearing barkcloth coats and after expressing interest in them I was sold one that fitted, for a small sum. When they become old and worn, the bark gets fluffy and the appearance from a distance is like brown, hairy wool.

The chief was quite young and was obviously the type who liked a good party. My arrival gave him an excellent excuse and he announced that in the evening there would be a grand kanjet of all the longhouses to take place on the area outside his quarters.

It was due to start about nine and soon after seven o'clock my companion from Long Sungai Anai turned up and said he had located his sister. She was standing behind him and out of the light of the oil lamp. When she advanced I saw that it was the same woman with whom I had travelled on the timber boat in Sarawak, stayed with at Long Bulan, travelled on to Long Jawi and had intended to go through to Long Nawang with, before the intervention of the police sergeant.

It was a happy coincidence and she was very interested to hear about the long route I had had to take to get here, instead of being able to follow her from Long Jawi over the border. I was equally interested to discover that her occupation was to travel round Kenyah communities in Sarawak and Kalimantan to assist with childbrith. Remembering that she was the only Muslim native living in the interior that I had met or heard of, I wondered if her role, prompted by Sarawakian authorities, did not have any additional significance to it. Native people would not have been able to pay much for her services and the motivation needed to travel tiringly over great distances on the off-chance of finding a pregnant native who required her help seemed to be thin on the grounds of public spirit only. Thinking back, I recalled how she had said a brief goodbye to her husband and family at Long Bulan, having only stayed there for two nights before heading for Indonesia. Later when the police sergeant had returned to Long Jawi from upriver, somehow her husband had been with him. A rum business, but early on I had given up trying to work out how people and information seemed to move so quickly from place to place.

The brother was beaming at the coincidence of the reunion and took the opportunity to mention again that he had been to Singapore and Johor Baru. To commemorate the event they were anxious I should chew some betel nut with them. I did not want to be churlish so I complied. The previous time I had tried it I had felt so sick that I had lain down to recover and had been subject to native revival techniques that included having leaves stuck on my face while people fanned me with banana leaves. I did not want to go through this again, so I concentrated on not swallowing any of the juice and followed their custom of squirting a jet of red saliva through the floorboards.

As zero hour for the party approached we were oiled with some borak and the tinkling sapes started warming up outside.

A huge crowd had assembled, completely filling the main area and extending on both sides down the verandah. I estimated there were about three hundred and fifty people. The music was supplied by six expert sape players. Without amplifiers so many instruments were needed to produce the volume necessary for the occasion. Two bamboo xylophones completed the musical ensemble. The opening sequence started with thirty-three girls filing in from the darkened ends of the verandah. They all wore the multicoloured aprons open at the back to mid-thigh and short jackets flared over their hips; beads and accessories jangled. Most of them had split ears with rings dangling. Their hair which normally hung loose was arranged under intricately woven rotan head bands.

I was sitting next to the chief who had gathered his hair into a pony tail and looked more like a hippie than ever.

It immediately became obvious that this was a troupe which had put in considerable practice. The normal slow dance of girls in a longhouse consists of ten girls who work their way round a big circle shuffling one foot forward and then the other, but pausing momentarily in mid-step, chanting all the while and encouraging people to join the line.

Here, however, thirty-three girls were forming, breaking and re-forming lines and groups in a complicated routine of steps and arm waving. One second they looked as if they were all polishing windows, and half would step back, the other half across, then down and twist, up, wiggle, down, step, wave and so on.

When the girls had finished, the individual dances started. My friend from Sungai Anai performed an excellent renditon of the final lopping off of somebody's head. After the preliminary twists and turns representing stalking, he did a mad rush and with a blood-curdling whoop swished his parang through an imaginary neck.

His sister, the midwife from Long Bulan, was also highly accomplished in the technical aspects of her dance, and earned a big round of applause. One costume was a complete leopard skin that two of the men bedecked themselves in, performing a sequence that involved a lot of sudden jumps in the air.

The evening wore on into the early hours and was a great success. For dancing skill and sheer enthusiasm it was the highlight of all entertainments I had seen. Perhaps it was the large numbers, perhaps it was because the headman obviously still regarded the custom as important and something to be encouraged, that made it so enjoyable. Initially I had thought the dancing was going to be for my benefit but at the end I was certain that it would have taken place anyway. I could see from the newness of the costumes and the ability of the musicians and dancing girls that this type of evening was held regularly.

The next day in another demonstration of his organising ability, the chief asked if I would take a group photograph of the whole village. The whole population of about five hundred was rounded up into a nearby field.

Throughout my stay ripe fruit continued to be brought in basketfuls: buah esow, buah abung, similar to lychee, rambutan and buah agglarong with its deliciously scented skin.

I strolled around the longhouses recognising some of the people from the dance night and on one verandah I encountered a crone with her hand held in a begging manner, but it was not for alms. Behind her was a little girl removing lice from her hair and placing them in the upturned hand. I went and inspected the little pile of executed lice, whereupon she let out a toothless cackle followed by a jet of red saliva from her wad of betel nut and leaves.

My plan was to bypass Datadian and go up the Iwan river, but as nobody was intending to go that way I decided to buy my own boat and become my own captain. I also purchased paddles, steel tipped poles and poles with hooks on the end for pulling myself along on the overhanging branches growing along the river bank. The chief insisted I would be heading for disaster. He said it required at least two people in the boat when negotiating fast water. I accepted these points, but was at least determined to try. The morning of my intended departure I came down to the bank with my bag and found a large audience to watch the antics of this 'madman'. I put my bag in the boat, got in and immediately water started pouring in; the boat had been sabotaged. Glancing about to try to spot a guilty look from the culprit, I soon realised that I had not a hope, and could only accept the chief's offer to row me to Datadian where I could walk to Long Lemiliu on the Iwan.

A Kenyah farmer in the Baram, with dog, waits for a lift across the river.

11

Trekking with Penans

We pulled our boat up the shallow sandbank at Datadian and set out to locate the camat, or district officer. After an hour's search we discovered that he had fallen asleep in the general store and had been locked in by the store proprietor. There was a large padlock on the outside of the door, and after we knocked, the camat started hammering from the inside demanding to be let out. Another twenty minutes passed before we released him, looking dishevelled. He thanked us briefly and invited us into his house. He turned out to be a Kenyah, although Datadian is a big Kayan centre and the capital of Kayan Hilir.

The camat spoke a little English, which made things easier and through him I thanked the chief and his men. Hengki Ba was the camat's name, and after he had regained his composure I found him very good company, as well as helpful. He was big for a native, about six feet and well built. An imposing figure, he had a gentle manner, and was treated with great respect by the natives. Being a natural leader, getting locked in the store had in no way lessened his ultimate self-possession.

He took me up to his office, located at the top of a steep hill and while I studied some of the maps on the wall, he studied my pass. Then we went down to see the military representative who likewise studied my pass and snapped a chop on it. He gave me his visitor's book to sign, which had only three other names, all local, in it. Finally the policeman had his turn, and affixed his mark to my pass.

Back to the camat's home where his wife had prepared a big meal

Blowpiper in action. The Penans are astonishingly accurate hunters with their silent and deadly weapons.

of pig and chili, rice and brinjals. I explained during the meal that I intended to walk to Long Lemiliu, and if he would be kind enough to point me in the right direction I felt I could make my way there. If I got lost I needed to head due west until I reached the Iwan river and then I could follow that to the kampong. Hengki was horrified.

'You are certain to be killed if you are seen walking on your own by the natives.'

'Why is that?'

'They won't understand what you are doing and will shoot you with blowpipes.'

'Charming.'

In the short time I had been with the natives I knew that they were inclined to slight hyperbole so after further discussion I said I would take the risk.

At this point he put his money where his mouth was, and offered a free armed escort with him leading, if I would consent to be accompanied. It was an offer I could not refuse, and after he had gathered four men with ancient rifles (from Long Jawi) we set off.

We reached Long Lemiliu just before nightfall, and were immediately offered rice soaked in borak, and a white chalky substance cooked in bamboos. Whenever the men walked across the kampong they took their guns with them. It all seemed rather unnecessary, so I asked the camat the real reason for such precautions.

'This village has been attacked several times by bandits in the night. They roam around in the jungle and kill people they meet.'

It sounded unlikely. In Sarawak I was told that the Indonesians paid a bounty to bring in dead or alive communists and other undesirables. Perhaps this loose form of policing had had bad repercussions, making gamekeepers turn poachers. I did not probe the camat on this, but left him presiding over a court session involving a marital dispute, while I was given an armed escort to visit the sick people in the village to dispense juicy-looking vitamin tablets. I returned to find Hengki giving his verdict. The wife had not been allowed to divorce her husband, who had been discovered in an illicit relationship with a girl from Long Sungan. A few more disputes were settled before I endeavoured to persuade him I needed only one man to walk with me to Long Kelawit further upriver. They would not hear of this, as one man would be frightened to return on his own, and anyway they said they had to use a boat for the first part of the trip so I was again stuck with four people.

We poled, heaved and pushed our way upstream for several hours while every few hundred yards I caught sight of a perfectly good path running beside the river. Finally we arrived at a farmhouse, where the boat was obviously destined to be loaded up with farm produce, so we started walking.

Now that the heavy work of poling was over I tried to persuade at least two of my guides to drop out. I emphasised the point so strongly that it created a crowd of inquisitive people wondering what was happening. My guides, much to my annoyance, told them I was trying to get rid of them because I was frightened that they would attack me. It was an unintentionally good ploy for although they did not know that I understood, I felt bound to regain the initiative, and so reluctantly told them to get on with our march.

The path was very complicated and undoubtedly on my own I would have got lost, but four men were definitely unnecessary. We walked for several hours, passing eggs placed in bamboo containers for the spirits and enjoyed some fruit from trees that had previously belonged to the villagers at Long Lisan who had moved from this village about ten years before.

As the hours passed our column got spread out and on hearing a hornbill rattling nearby I waited for the first man to catch me up. I indicated the noise and he immediately murmured '*babi*' (pig) and went stalking into the bush with his blowpipe. The hornbill obviously saw him, and flapped into the tree directly over my head. The man soon came back, and I tried to point out his pig in the tree. He still could not see it, so I borrowed the blowpipe and endeavoured to blast it with a dart. I took a mighty puff, nearly blew my eyeballs out of their sockets and failed miserably to get the range.

I tell this little story to indicate the lack of prowess that the Kayans and Kenyahs generally show in the jungle. In the same way that most town people do not endlessly go for long country walks, these village people usually prefer to remain close to their longhouses and their farms, with a little fishing thrown in.

In the afternoon it rained briefly and the men pulled out of their bags cunningly designed waterproof covers made from a narrow bladed palm. These covers fitted exactly over their heads and baggage on their backs. It covered just the parts that needed to be kept dry and still left both hands free.

Before nightfall and a short distance from Long Kelawit we had to cross one of the enchanting little rocky rivers that constantly meander through the jungle in the highland regions. The sun had come out again and for a quarter of an hour we used the river to wash and bathe in. The coolness of the water worked on tired muscles, and the variegated patches of light filtering through the foliage produced vivid streaks of rainbow where the spray fanned from behind a rock. I lay with my body just submerged and with the clean clear water trickling past, and wished I could stay longer.

It was only a short distance from this river to Long Kelawit, which I was surprised to see was laid out around a large grass square in English village tradition. Each side of the square was about one hundred and fifty yards long, with a longhouse running the full length. Further smaller storage huts were set behind one of the longhouses on the side where the Kelawit river joined the Iwan. It seemed prosperous with masses of bulging fruit trees, plenty of big banana plantations and the whole area well tended. The people looked fit and well fed, but I had been told that the headman was hoping to move to near Tanjung Selor. I mentioned this to my headman who seemed very surprised that I should know and at first seemed reluctant to admit it in front of the people sitting around. Big moves often cause rifts in communities; while the main bulk will follow the headman, breakaway groups will set off elsewhere on their own.

From Long Kelawit I was again faced with the 'local tax' problem. I began to realise that their insistence that I take four men was a way of my paying toll for passing through their territory. On this stretch the guides were a diverse group; one was a fairly old man and two were middle aged. One of these I thought was half mad because of his unblinking staring eyes and strange way of walking. He soon proved to be a phenomenal worker. For nine hours he toiled solidly and his incredibly muscular body was a tribute to his hard working ways. The fourth member was a cocky youth whose job was to steer the boat from the back, cook and generally act as a dogsbody. It was a much easier job than the endless round of paddling, poling and pulling with the long hook-ended poles, and I was surprised that the old man did not take this task.

I only needed to paddle from the cross-legged position, even in their hypnotic rhythm, for a couple of hours to know how tiring it was. Their rhythm was a hard stroke ending with a click of the paddles on the side of the boat, followed by a lighter shorter stroke where only half the paddle was dipped into the water, and then the hard stroke again. We picked up some horse mango floating down the river and stopping on a small island in the middle of the stream ate them for lunch. It was a short stop of twenty minutes, and then we were off again in the same routine. We stopped briefly in mid-afternoon to try to catch some fish. The old man throwing the net got it caught in the river bed; thinking a stone was responsible he dived down to release it, and surfaced clutching a river turtle. These creatures, which grow to more than four feet long, have a terrifying bite like a piranha fish and natives are very careful to keep away from the front end. With this precaution in mind I picked it up to have a look at it with the head facing away, and was rewarded with a remarkably powerful jet of black slime being squirted from its rear end.

We spent the night at Long Ikeng where there was an old hut formerly used as a farmhouse. Old fruit trees still bore some fruit that the monkeys had not eaten. We supplemented the fruit with rice and fern soup. Some old bamboo gongs which had been used for scaring off monkeys lay in a corner. Also propped against a wall was a long, thin metal spoke used for hollowing out blowpipes.

The river opposite this old farmhouse had a terrible plague of river flies, far worse than the sandflies that inhabited most of the rocky river banks. They descended on naked flesh in a swarm and left a sizeable lump. It was impossible to wash there, and furthermore it was an unpleasant muddy bank with a short beach of leaf mould covered in fine-grained sand leading down to the murky, muddy bed of the main river. My aversion to walking barefoot in muddy water grew stronger the longer I travelled through the interior. Now I kept imagining that a river turtle might clamp his teeth into my toes whenever I went in. Near occupied longhouses unwelcome inhabitants of the river stay above or below the main bathing area, but in an unused stretch of river anything could be reposing in the muddy depths.

From Long Ikeng we crossed the river and struck out westwards towards the Pasok river where the Penans live. As soon as we left the river valley we were faced with steep hills and had to walk along the narrow pebbly streams, often up a very steep gradient. Constantly having to climb under or over fallen logs and tangled masses of vines or plants is tiring work, as is concentrating on not slipping on the damp green lichen covering the rocks, and wriggling under hazards with a pack on one's back.

The course of the Pasok river was fascinating, for it descended through a myriad course of waterfalls, rockpools, and short marshy patches. The jungle here was so dense that it was twilight in the middle of the day. Huge trees formed an impenetrable canopy overhead. That Penans were near was evident from cut sago palms lying near the banks of the stream; and after about four hours we met the first ones. A man and his wife, attired in ragged loin-cloths, were searching for fruit trees and after wishing them a good day we carried on.

The Kenyahs were at pains to point out to me that my rudimentary grasp of Indonesian was going to be useless with the Penans as they only spoke their own language with a little knowledge of Kenyah.

If all else failed I decided to take the advice of Emang, who once told me that natives who had never heard a word of English could still somehow understand it. I had asked for clarification on this ambiguous point. He explained that the sound of English words, and the way it was spoken, were such that the natives could understand what was being said. I had experimented with this once or twice and sure enough if after the first attempt they looked blank one merely raised volume and intensity and they understood at once. It was excellent. I am sure this must have given rise to the bad image of English colonialists, who in the eyes of an independent observer would have been behaving thoroughly boorishly when they were merely communicating in a simple Esperanto.

However, when we reached the small Penan community camped on the Kihan river I tried some of the dialect I had learned up the Linau in Sarawak. It was the same, and while the Kenyahs communicated with hand signals and pidgin Kenyah I held simple conversation in their own language. One up to the white man. It turned out the Penan Busang and Penan Apoh where I had been in Sarawak were only five days' walk away from here and were part of the same group as the Penan Kihan. They were anxious to know who the new headman was at Long Tangit, and very pleased when I could tell them; I had become a link in the bush telegraph and felt very gratified. This promising start led to a warm welcome. I was placed in their public hut while every family brought the best of what they had to offer. I picked my way through a range of jungle delicacies while chatting with the amicable headman. The Kenyah guides hurriedly traded some tobacco for a mat and left again.

All the people here were friendly in a way that completely set the Penans aside from the other tribes I had met. Lacking shyness, they offered help, anxious to please just for the sake of it. Several young men immediately volunteered to show me the way on my next section. It was to be eight days' walking through the jungle without coming to a longhouse. This prospect would have daunted the Kenyahs, but the Penans were happy to go. I selected just two men, without a murmur of protest about needing at least four.

They had the usual abundant collection of skilfully woven rotan mats and baskets made by the women, one of whom caught my eye. She was unusual looking, with slightly ginger hair, a very pale skin, and pink nipples. All seemed a jolly crowd and, after I had eaten, the headman arranged for the girls to dress themselves up and do a little dance.

This encampment of Penans was more permanent than the lean-tos which they usually build. The individual little huts were set high on stilts with banana trees growing among them.

Throughout my time with the Penans on Sungai Kihan I was treated with unblemished hospitality by everybody there. It was a community where I would have liked to have spent more time, and the experience prompted me to visit Penan groups in Sarawak, which I mention later. The Sungai Kihan people told me the rare rhinoceros survived in the area. Just in case one should be nearby, I decided to take a slow route to Long Mesahan, not following any of the well trodden paths. Most tracks anyway on this route are practically completely overgrown as Long Mesahan is now deserted and coastal supplies have to be flown in to Datadian, which makes the interior of Kalimantan most interesting and was one of the reasons why I had come to this area. The constant depopulation of former villages means that wildlife is becoming more abundant and trekking less easy.

Muda Tingun and Laping Sohia were my two Penan guides on this interesting stretch through primary jungle. We set off down the Sungai Kihan in a small boat, and when the water became too rough we landed on the bank, walked for a couple of hours, and then picked up another boat that had been left in the bushes and so continued down to Long Kihan.

Long Kihan was where the Penans had previously been camped and several trees with ripe pomaloes were located where they had lived. We collected the ones that had freshly fallen into water and made our way to the Sungai Suhen, which is almost opposite the Kihan. There we met some more Penans who were collecting durian fruit from a big tree nearby. They were on their way to Datadian to sell baskets and mats. With our enormous stocks of fruit we rested on an open stretch of bank and feasted ourselves. I was astonished to see how many durians each man ate; after consuming six each they wrapped the extra pips in wild banana leaves for later consumption. This habit of gorging themselves on durian would happen every time we came across a tree. About an hour after consuming them, the gases from the fruit would set to work and for the next hour they would be merrily farting. I used to time my stints in front during these periods.

Not following tracks, we were constantly bending, diverting and cutting prickling creepers and vines that blocked our way; an endless pattern of following small streams and crossing over a hill to follow another stream. It was extremely tiring because we were never able just to walk. Either it was stumbling over uneven pebbly stones in a river bed or scrambling up the hill and down the other side. Occasionally we would come to an open patch where a big tree had fallen and the light penetrating through had enabled grass and small plants to grow on the jungle floor. An immense variety of orchids grew on the tree trunks and high up in the branches; their beautiful waxen flowers often littered the ground.

Small patches of seemingly raked ground were evidently produced by a type of ground bird. The Penans tried to explain to me how and why the birds made these patches but I could not fully understand.

Above all, the hunting was exciting. It was exhilarating because it was done in the most primitive way possible: one man with his spear against a wild animal. Innumerable times one of the men would motion us to stop with a thin noise made by pursing his lips and sucking. The form was immediately to crouch and keep still, then the man would point to where the animal was. If it was not a wild boar we merely sat and watched it; a wild boar, however, was fair game, and one of the Penans would slip away like a shadow to stalk it. Several times the man behind me would disappear without my ever realising it. I would see him one minute crouched on the ground, then turning back two seconds later he was nowhere to be seen. During this time the other one would point out his friend's progress and without his aid I could never see where he was.

Writing this now I can feel the excitement as I watched my first successful stalk with the shadowy figure creeping nearer and nearer to a huge boar rootling near the bank of a stream. Slowly, slowly the Penan raised his spear in a javelin-thrower's posture and made a mad dash forward. The boar looked up with a startled grunt and then the spear thudded into its body. The spear had entered its intestines and the boar galloped away up the bank. My inclination was to go rushing after it with wild whoops, but Tingun indicated quickly to stay still. To run after it would make it run further.

Cautiously, we followed the path it had taken into the jungle. At the first brush against a tree the spear had come out with a large coil of intestine attached to it. Initially the trail was easy as the spear had ripped a big hole and pieces of gut were deposited along the route it had taken. When this trail ended we followed the blood trail where it had brushed against green leaves; where the blood dripped on the ground it was immediately absorbed and impossible to follow.

Several times they almost lost the trail, but suddenly a grunt and rustle of undergrowth ahead indicated we were getting close. We came across the small hollow the pig had been lying in; a big pool of blood was on the bottom.

As stealthily as in the original stalk the two men crept ahead. Suddenly the front one saw it. The boar had doubled back to the stream and was lying against a big rock, panting.

Both of them manoeuvred into position and with a signal charged down a short incline. The boar was up in a flash, still very much alive, and with its final fighting spirit endeavoured to lunge at Sohia with its wicked, eight inch tusks. Sohia sprang like a cat to one side, at the same time burying his spear behind its foreleg. The boar let out a sound between a grunt and a squeal and flicked round to intercept Tingun who was trying to aim his spear into the other side. He plunged it in just as the beast charged him. The first spear had already killed the boar and its dying rush at Tingun ended with it falling dead at his feet.

At this point I appeared, and heartily congratulated both of them. I estimated the weight of the pig to be between three hundred and three hundred and fifty pounds. The men quickly cut out the best pieces and left the bulk of the carcase lying where it had ended its days.

We made our way back to our packs. I would have had trouble finding them, back-tracking carefully, but the Penans took a short-cut. Their sense of direction was phenomenal and they never bothered with the little cuts in the trees as other natives do.

Soon after picking our packs up we made a shelter for the night. These shelters used to take them forty minutes to make — a simple lean-to with a front flap tied together with creepers and covered in big leaves. It was quite waterproof. Nearly every night it rained yet we never got wet. Watching them making the shelter and preparing a fire from damp wood, I could see that they were enjoying themselves as much as I was. It made all the difference to be with natives who were happy to be just travelling through the jungle stopping to look at anything interesting, collecting fruit, hunting and finding our way. Nothing was 'susah', or difficult; nobody was 'takut' or frightened. I thought of the average guide who, however politely patient, is still anxious to get the job over and the money in his hand. The Penan guides had volunteered to come without pay-ment and only after I asked them how much they wanted did they say that they would be happy with whatever I gave them.

Leaves were placed under our lean-to and then we put our mats on top. Fires burned well although most of the wood was damp to start with. Initially the Penans shaved away the damp outside of the wood and used the drier shavings on the inside of the stick. Our newly-killed chunks of boar were boiled with fern soup and we fin-ished off with salted durian. The remaining meat was smoked on

wooden skewers and used during the day.

The nights lying on the ground in the middle of the jungle always made me feel a little uneasy. One seemed to be completely vulnerable. Tingun and Sohia were happy to let the fire burn out, but I used to keep it stoked up throughout the night, both against the chill at this altitude, and as a form of reassurance.

One night I awoke to hear an animal, almost certainly a pig, rootling nearby. The fire had burned low, so there was only a very faint glow. Everywhere there was complete darkness with the occasional drip of water on to the leaves, and the startlingly close rummaging sent goose-pimples down my back. I sat up to try and ascertain the exact location, and as I did so Tingun asked, 'What is it, Tuan?'

My answer, if I could have said it, would have been, 'Well, I was going to ask you that.'

Even though one can be fairly certain it is a pig, the inability to see anything and the sensation of complete helplessness give all sorts of fuel to the imagination. I could easily understand the legends of hobgoblins, tree spirits and jungle sprites. The loneliness, the uncertainty, the massive clammy void of jungle had to have some ulterior forces living and existing to lend some explanation to it all.

I always felt relief when dim points of light began to show through the canopy above. We would get up, roll up our mats, have a quick dip in the stream, which was cold but refreshing and eat the remains of what we had had the previous night. It would be cold and it was generally very insubstantial. This was the low point of the day. If I ever found myself missing something it was a hot drink before setting off. Invariably for the first hour, with my pack rubbing sore patches through my damp shirt, I was uncomfortable and slightly dizzy; but with the first sweat starting I immediately felt better; and the daily spartan diet on top of hard exercise had me feeling fitter and fitter. It showed me how much unnecessary food I usually ate, and why I spent so much of my time lacking in energy. It was interesting to discover that instead of getting run down as the trip progressed the effect of less food and hard exercise made me stronger and more energetic. Apart from that first hour I spent the whole day feeling physically alert and inwardly relaxed; it was an ideal combination.

However this feeling of confidence cracked as soon as I succumbed to an ailment. The high incidence of fever in Kalimantan inevit-

A Penan couple on the march — cooking pot, the woman's clothing and even a wristwatch belie their primitive way of life.

ably affected me, and on the three occasions I was laid up I felt appalling.

When we came to a young fruit tree Tingun and Sohia would cut it down. It seemed a wasteful way of collecting enough fruit to eat on the spot and for the small amount we could carry on with us. Usually natives shin up fruit trees and cut down suitable branches. Perhaps Tingun and Sohia assumed that they would not be taking that route again so that it did not matter.

Jackfruit and its various sub-species were in abundance; these had to be collected where they had fallen and the rotten part cut away. We came across at least two durian trees a day.

Without rice, we used the heart of the sago palm. They were expert at selecting just the right part of the stem to cut and with a minimum of work would cut a neat sliver in the palm and extract the round white sticks of sago. They tasted completely neutral but two or three sticks were a good substitute for the missing bulk of rice.

One afternoon we were eating fruit when a storm which had been gradually building up reached its full fury. The wind ripped through the trees on the slope and almost at once, as if an earthquake had struck, dead trees and big branches started falling all around us. The noise was stupendous and it was impossible to see from which direction the falling timber was coming. We abandoned our packs and ran helter skelter like frightened rabbits. A huge buttress tree provided a haven while the holocaust passed as quickly as it had started. Again this unpredicted incident almost seemed like an angry spirit letting off steam. We returned to our bags, which were covered with a big branch, and set off again.

Further on another big tree fell bringing down two other trees with it. The noise of cracking, splintering timber was tremendous in the overall stillness of the jungle.

One afternoon was brightened up when a large monitor lizard flashed across our route. Equally fast, Sohia dropped his pack and sprinted after it with his spear. The pace he maintained barefoot over and under every conceivable hazard in pursuit of this fleeing creature was phenomenal. It ended with them both launching themselves off a rock, at the same time, towards a large pool. In mid air Sohia jabbed his spear into the scaly hide. Splosh! The lizard was better under water than Sohia, and lodged underneath a rock. Frantic underwater jabs with his spear were merely a consolation to his pride at losing the prey.

On and on we continued, ignoring most of the pigs we spotted, but I did make one attempt to kill one myself. I stalked the boar with utmost care for some time, but after a wide detour was unaware that it had moved position. I thought I was crawling towards it when in fact it was calmly rootling to one side of me. It soon saw me and trundled across the stream. Tingun, who had seen what was going to happen, had tried to intercept it, but his spear whistled through its bristle and so it joined the statistics of the ones that got away.

The only time I saw the Penans react with great animation was when I had a large furry caterpillar on my hat. Tingun pointed it out with great feeling and even after it had been disposed of, he made a noise of revulsion while he shuddered. He insisted I wash my hat, making sure that I did not touch the part where the caterpillar had been. He indicated that it was highly poisonous.

Two extra large hills marked our approach to the Punjungan river and having reached it we had a hard job to ford it. The water was running very fast. With the bottom half of my bag submerged, and only with the use of poles to support myself was I able gingerly to ease my way across.

We walked a short distance along the river bank and noticed signs of former habitation, in particular the brilliant white of coffee bush flowers. Nearby was the Mesahan river. Walking up the bank we saw a whole kampong of buildings and fruit trees but not a single person. Tingun and Sohia, however, were certain that four people were staying there. They had read one of the little jungle signs left by four people on the outskirts of this deserted village saying that they were there. So as not to alarm them we left our spears on the outskirts and started to walk around.

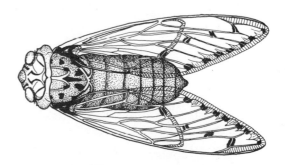

Even the insects are ornamental.   155

12

King Cobra

We were met with the extraordinary sight of a recently evacuated community. Everything required in the day-to-day life of the natives was still there: boats, parangs, rice winnowing equipment, baskets, hats, mats and so on.

One of the longhouses had some sleeping dogs outside which growled threateningly at us, and assuming this was where the four people were holed up, we knocked. An excited discussion broke out following this knock; they talked to Tingun and Sohia through the locked door and after a long exchange they cautiously opened the door. We must have looked pretty harmless for they quickly ushered us in. There were three men and a woman. They seemed to be the remnants of this previously one-thousand-people kampong. In fact they had merely returned to collect some gongs and other valuables, including a sack of coffee beans.

Once we had got over the formalities, we settled into a lively atmosphere. Tingun and Sohia spent their time mixing up the poison for blowpipe dart tips, I went off fishing with one of the Kenyahs and in between times we ate what fruit had been left by the monkeys. The husband of the woman was shaven headed and quite obviously a joker. He kept the company roaring with laughter, and even his facial expressions and manner of speech were amusing on their own. On the second day Sohia came down with fever. By then I had arranged to continue with the Kenyahs who were heading for Long Saan.

I saw a bit of bush telegraph in action as paper messages that had

Kenyah mother and child. The beadwork on baby carriers and other items is so fine that they have become collectors' items.

157

been brought from the coast were given to the Penans to relay on to a longhouse at Long Kelawit. It was pure chance we had met the Kenyahs and the information they were handing over would get to its destination very quickly. I could imagine that the same information travelling by the 'quickest' method, the plane to Datadian and then upriver by boat, would probably arrive later than this remote transaction and lead people to gasp, 'How did they know?'

The expression 'eating like a pack of dogs' was well demonstrated at feeding time for their hunting pack. A large container of pigs' guts and bones and mashed unripe papaya was boiled up and then poured into a trough while the dogs feverishly snapped, growled and slurped up the food as quickly as possible. At the end their stomachs were widely distended. They were particularly skilful at splitting up rock-hard pigs' bones. In the evenings we had a fire on the verandah and the dogs would lie practically in the flames, always in strict order of precedence. I enjoyed watching the pecking order of their hierarchy.

The Kenyah woman had black hair that when released from the rotan headband flowed down to her feet. She was not a short woman, and kept her hair cut at ankle level. Every night she rubbed coconut oil into it to keep it shining attractively.

Unlike the Ibans, the people of the interior have a custom which dictates that guests eat first. I used to find it slightly annoying. The food for the whole family would be laid out and I would be invited to eat first while everybody sat round watching and waiting until I finished so that they could spring on the remains. The first day at Long Mesahan they insisted on this, but later abandoned it for the more convivial general eating. (One could then select a tasty morsel without feeling so guilty.)

With so many abandoned objects I would have liked to have bought many of the things there, but of course the problem of transport which prevented them from taking the goods with them, also hampered me. I did, however, get a leopard skin cover used in the kanjet dance, and the woman very generously gave me a string of blue and white stone beads which the Kenyahs and Kayans seem to value very highly.

The third day Tingun and Sohia left. As they disappeared into the jungle I felt quite sad; we had formed a friendly relationship in the days we had been together.

Almost as soon as they were out of sight the Kenyahs started to explain how 'susah', or difficult, the next part of the route would be. For them it was, as they were carrying about a hundred pounds each. A final fire was lit and some small shells from the river were heated and ground up to be used as lime for their betel nut chewing. The dogs were given an enormous trough of food, and with their stomachs bulging, we set off on a well cleared path. It seemed extraordinary to be leaving a large kampong of several longhouses complete with boats tied up at the river bank, and coconut and fruit trees bulging with fruit, but not a soul in sight.

Our route was not directly to Long Saan. We made a detour to Long Pahai, a two-door longhouse in a very remote spot. The two families, consisting of about fifteen people in total, had no modern conveniences at all. They lit their fires or their cheroots with a flint and ball of mushroom shavings. On striking the flint, a spark would start the shavings smouldering and from this they could light a fire or a cheroot. The dried shavings were remarkably flammable.

Naturally I enquired how these people came to be in such a remote place. They explained that three years earlier they had made the long trip up the Iwan, building a boat specially for the trip, going across the border and on to Long Moh on the Baram. Then down to Miri where they had worked for two years. When they decided to return they came back the same way, recovered their boat from the bushes on the banks of the Iwan and made the long trip back to Long Mesahan. Disconsolately they had wandered round their deserted village and finding no clues as to where everybody had gone, they had started a small longhouse of their own a few hours' walk away.

They now of course knew that everybody had moved to Antutan on the lower Kayan but they preferred to stay where they were. The advantage of living in isolated areas was the abundance of wild game as a food source and invariably the more isolated people were physically bigger and stronger than those in the more crowded longhouses near the coast.

The shaven headed joker had told me before we set off that in the evening he would have an attack of 'demam; or fever, and sure enough at six-thirty sharp he started shivering and pouring with sweat. He crawled under a cover and we waited for the attack to pass. In the meantime I introduced the others to the card game 'Snap'. They took to it very quickly, and had no problems matching English milkmen, postmen and farmers together.

The men carrying gongs decided that they were too heavy to carry any further and left them in a hut to be collected later. This seems to be the way they move things; in a series of relays across the jungle, only taking as much as they could carry over the rough terrain. I thought what an enormous difference a helicopter would make. Thousands of man hours would be saved.

With the shaven headed joker recovered we set off once more. As we left, all the longhouse people shouted 'Snap', and away we went. I left the 'Snap' pack with them and no doubt at this very moment the excited shout is probably ringing out of the longhouse.

The leeches, I remember, were so terrible that they seemed to spring out from the bushes as well as the ground. We fashioned some simple scrapers out of wood to flick off the leeches as soon as they attached themselves. Some jungle manuals suggest burning them off and rubbing salt into them, but to start this process would mean about half the day was spent laboriously lighting matches or wasting salt. However what really causes a leech to squirm in agony is to be immersed in red saliva from betel nut chewing.

There were wide, impressive views of grass-covered hills and deep plunging valleys. The heavy loads of the Kenyahs meant we were continually stopping to rest and our progress was very slow. The first night was spent in an old shelter near the path.

The second day we reached the Punjungan river again at a spot where a boat should have been. There was no sign of it, so one of the Kenyahs, a big strong fellow, plunged into the river which was very rough and swam the fifty yards to the other bank. He reached it about a mile downstream and after making his way back fortunately discovered the missing boat.

On the way we had passed near Long Maring, and they explained to me that at one time their longhouse had been located here.

'How long ago?' I asked.

'Long time already.'

'Can you tell me all the places that you can remember where your community has been.'

He responded to this well and the following list shows how their history is passed on verbally. Each place represents approximately thirty years.

MUDONG MERBAY	LONG PUSAH
DEPONG KUHAT	LONG BOH
LONG MARING	LONG MESAHAN
PUTONG	ANTUTAN (JUST MOVED HERE)
LONG ULUK	

Winding our way through the high grasslands near Long Saan, it seemed like an African safari. There were frequent long views across rolling, jungle-clad hills and light green patches of coarse grass. No trees grow where this grass takes root, and it seems as if all padi fields after they have been exhausted give way to this choking grass.

The pack of ten dogs constantly caught the scent of an animal and rushed off in a baying mob until they were scarcely audible. Half an hour later they would come panting back to wait for the next scent. It was impossible to tell them to conserve their energy for a proper hunt. Their disappointed faces seemed to say, 'Why didn't you follow us after that pig?'

Late in the day we arrived at Long Saan. This kampong was in the most impressive location I have ever seen, two thousand feet above sea level and eight hundred feet above the Punjungan river. The walk from the village to the river was down a steep path running down the mountainside. Immediately before descending this gradient the path ran along a narrow ridge that gave views of the Punjungan river valley on one side and the Saan river valley on the other. The Saan valley had a backdrop of massive limestone caves which the Kenyahs use as burial chambers, while the Punjungan valley was dotted with steep hills crowned by the strangely shaped Batu Bulu. Trekking along this ridge was like flying in an aircraft.

Our walk had been tiring, and on arrival at the headman's quarters I felt like sleeping and sleeping, but this was quite impossible. A bottle of Chinese brandy was produced and after the statutory draining of the glass a couple of times, I was keener than ever to lie down. I was on the point of suggesting it when the headman insisted that I take part in a football game that was about to start.

There was no getting out of it, and for the next hour, half drunk and exhausted, I endeavoured to put on a good performance. They tend to assume that any European must be good at football, and even in one of the government officers in Sarawak I was asked what league I played in. There was no question that I either might not play football or not be in a league at all. It would seem that England is now known more for its football than anything else.

The headman was much the best player on the field; I wondered if this was how he had secured his position as head of the village, because apart from his commanding presence on the field he did not seem to be in the authoritative mould that tends to distinguish most village chiefs.

Long Saan was another community in the grip of an exodus. In the previous five years the population had dwindled from one thousand to three hundred, and my subsequent exit was with some migrants.

It was instantly understandable that farming on such changing gradients must be very trying and imagine having to walk down eight hundred feet to go to the river.

A complicated system of split bamboos channelled delicious

sweet water from the mountain streams to the village. A certain amount of wet padi cultivation was practised, which I found surprising.

One evening the headman arranged a kanjet dance for me but instead of the usual entertainment the whole performance was a skit on the system. Only boys were in the long dance, walking round and round shouting instead of singing. The words were obviously crude from the general reaction. The banjoists strummed discordantly and by the time they started the individual efforts it was already eleven thirty p.m.

There followed a succession of longhouse comedians and comediennes taking off each other's dances. An old woman with a shield and parang pretended to stalk a victim and, screaming maniacally, rushed in for the kill. She was a horrifying sight and I was uncertain that she was not a little mad. Several boys pretended to be spastics trying to dance, and an old man repeatedly stood up and performed his party trick of putting a lighted match in his mouth.

One of them put a leopard skin over himself with the head over his head and pranced about. It was a different type of entertainment and I generally found it rather unsatisfactory. They were laughing at themselves in a rather unhealthy way.

Long Saan was a majestic location but I was not sad to leave it. The low morale of the inhabitants, probably caused by the people leaving, gave it a poor atmosphere.

Down by the river we waited several hours while all the boats were loaded up for the great move. Swarms and swarms of bees filled the air, and there was nowhere to escape. Most people jumped in the river periodically, but as soon as they got out their backs were black with the bees. I was wearing a shirt to begin with, which proved a mistake. Several bees got inside and, once restricted, started stinging. I was loath to swat them too hard in case I started a general madness among the others.

At zero hour the fifty people who were departing gathered round for a prayer session. Then with the sun at its zenith we dipped paddles and let the swishing current take us rushing down the river.

A sudden downpour caused a slight delay, because we had to stop, unload all the padi and dry it on mats laid out by the river bank. Progress then was very fast, shooting down the narrow channels between rocks lashed by flying spray.

Twice we had to unload and carry the boats past an impossible drop in levels. There was a certain amount of competition. The more daring crews would take a faster, more dangerous route, only to be overtaken in turn by another crew cutting an even finer course. It was a memorable sensation to see a patch of turbulent water ahead, knowing that we had to go through at one point, listening to the shouted debate from the paddlers on the best route and then plunging into the hazard.

The boat scraped against rocks, water churned over the sides, threatening innumerable times to capsize us while the natives exerted all their skills to bring us through unscathed.

As it was getting dark we arrived at Long Pua and I stayed at the headman's home. He was away, but his wife was holding the fort. It seemed that most of the boats were using Long Pua as a relay base, and were going back empty to pick up more things, while the ones continuing were loaded to the gunnels. Many of the women at Long Pua had large goitres, an affliction that rarely seemed to affect the interior people. The raised scar welts that everybody also seemed to have must have been caused by diet, perhaps too much fern soup. I acquired two on my shoulders, which gradually disappeared after I got back.

Fortunately the headman's wife was planning a trip to Long Punjungan and two days later I found myself comfortably ensconced in the middle of the boat with baggage on either side of me, four natives in the front and four at the back.

It was a relaxed trip. Some of the men tried fishing with a simple rod made with a stick of bamboo and a piece of red fruit attached to the line. They flicked this from side to side on to the surface of the water. It was meant to look like a juicy piece of fruit falling from a tree, and hopefully a fish would rise to impale itself on the hook. It never happened, so one of them resorted to using a net which was immediately successful. After several throws in different places, usually where a small stream joined the main river, but very often above a rapid, we had a respectable amount of fish in the boat.

Two more hours passed by with the current drifting us downstream. I was dozing with my umbrella up, watching the butterflies flapping around the baggage and generally feeling languid when a terrific hullabaloo started among the natives. I thought they had spotted a herd of pigs in the river, but they then started beating the water with their paddles and their excitement increased to panic level. I looked around in the direction of their interest, and was horrified to see a black snake about twelve feet long wiggling rapidly through the water straight towards me. Their frantic beating on the water with their paddles was not having the slightest effect, in fact it probably annoyed the snake even more. The snake was at the boat now and I had a split second to see its head rearing towards my leg with a big white patch on the underside of its jaw before I flashed my umbrella between my leg and its head. Its head struck the umbrella, and I jumped up and very nearly out of the other side of the boat. If I had ... The very next instant its head appeared from the other side of the boat. It came rearing up again and I was parrying it with my umbrella when two of the natives who had gained better positions over the baggage whacked it on the head with their paddles. It was only stunned and started to contort itself in the water. The natives scrambled back into position, and in the fastest piece of paddling I have ever seen spurted away from the most poisonous snake in Borneo — a king cobra.

I had seen several snakes in the jungle and even had a near brush with one when I had modestly selected a dense piece of foliage in which to relieve myself; but the prospect of being directly attacked by one had never occurred to me and gave me a healthy new respect for jungle hazards. Natives never go anywhere without their parangs strapped on, and from this incident I understood why.

The full significance and shock of how near I had come to disaster affected me after a few days when I had a hideous dream in which I relived a similar entanglement, only in the dream somehow I could not escape. I did not risk telling the natives about this dream otherwise there would have been a cease work and chicken's heads would have gone flying.

Long Punjungan meant a return to governmental administration. A camat was based there but he was not due back from a trip for a few days. The penghulu was laid up with a bad leg but I stayed in his spacious quarters. His wife had been entrusted by a visiting dispensary with an ancient hypodermic syringe with a range of different sized needles and a large quantity of penicillin for pumping into her husband. At least in Indonesia they allowed locals to administer medicaments.

Another resident in the penghulu's quarters was a blind man, who developed bad foot rot while I was there and after it failed to get better I saw the penghulu's wife selecting a suitable needle in order to give this poor chap a shot of penicillin.

The next time I saw the blind man being treated, a small boy was pouring petrol from an outboard engine on to his feet. He yowled and squirmed, but for some reason wanted this strange treatment to continue.

A Chinese trader was upriver buying rotan, and after he had loaded up I was hoping to get a lift downriver with him. The price, as expected from a Chinese trader, was ludicrous. I decided to wait until the camat returned.

In the meantime the penghulu's son, the school teacher and I went hunting with a pack of badly trained dogs. They rushed about barking at monkeys in the treetops, and after a monitor lizard had been decapitated they made a racket barking at its severed head flicking its tongue in and out. One day I went fishing with a net, and silenced a mob of sniggering children by landing a couple of fish with my first throw.

Evenings with the penghulu's family were a lot of fun. Card games and local games were played with great enthusiasm while the blind man sat singing or talking to a group of riveted children. The children used to hang on every word he spoke and I could see that with his incapacity he must have had hours for reflection in which to think up stories to tell.

The food I remember here was particularly varied and good. One sauce in particular, made from young coconut milk and crushed papaya, was superb.

Long Punjungan was fairly accessible, and local pastors had arranged for a simple church to be built where, among a relaxed congregation, babies urinated on the floor and dogs scrimmaged in the aisles.

When the camat returned I had a few words with him about going downstream. As usual the official was very helpful. He said to me, 'I'm writing a note for the Chinese rotan trader, ordering him to give you a lift, and you are not to pay him anything.'

This type of note was a reminder of the animosity felt by native officials against the Chinese in general, and traders in particular. As recently as 1968 the Chinese population had been wiped out in some isolated areas, and regularly orders go out for the Chinese to stop their trading activities upriver. It lasts for a while, and then slowly they return, tolerated mainly because nobody else seems capable of handling the overall organisation necessary.

The morning I left, the penghulu's daughters presented me with a package of food that would have lasted me a week. So I was able to placate the topee-toting Chinese and his men with pink rice cakes, bananas, papayas, salted fish, glutinous rice and two live chickens.

We zoomed downriver perched on a pile of rotan; at one point we stopped to pick up another boat concealed up a small stream. This was also loaded to the gunnels with rotan. The other stops on the way were to purchase some caged birds from native traders camped on the river bank.

The river is the core of the natives' existence. They rise in the morning, wash in it, excrete in it, draw their drinking water from it, fish from it and use it as a highway. It is a myth that the small stream located next to each longhouse is used only for drawing drinking water. Everywhere I went, small streams were used for all purposes.

13

Back to Tarakan

Arriving at Long Bia I again stayed with Ah-Ing, the Chinese patriarch, and had dinner with the missionary Frank Peters and his wife.

Marv, the other missionary pilot, had returned from Singapore with his plane and my inquiry about going to Datadian was answered with, 'As an expatriate you are bottom priority. I have no idea when you will be able to go.'

This seemed a reasonable enough principle, so I busied myself pig-sticking. At this time of the year, May, herds of pigs swim across the rivers when it is raining hard. This provides an easy way of killing the pigs, and for miles down the banks boats line up under the opposite bank waiting for a herd to enter the water.

In days past some might survive because they were faced with natives in paddle boats, but now Ah-Ing and his sons had a fleet of outboard engine boats that gave the pigs not a ghost of a chance. Every herd that entered the water would be allowed to swim to the middle of the river and then with a roar, a mass of boats sped from along the bank to intercept. Desperate races ensued to get to the herd first. Lightweight boats with fifty h.p. engines roaring at full power created a dangerous situation when they met the herd.

Standing in the bows with spears we would flash through the herd jabbing and spearing, concentrating on not falling in as we wheeled to avoid other boats doing the same thing, and desperately trying to haul aboard the pigs we had stuck. Most of the natives in paddle boats, who could be forgiven for the animosity they felt towards the power boats, would come paddling in as fast as they could to haul aboard pigs that had been bypassed.

The brief moments of action were marked by the squealing of the piglets, the outraged grunts of the boars as they struggled to get back to the far bank, floating pig carcases surrounded by pools of blood, engines roaring, excited shouting of the participants and the sickening 'snick' noises of the spears jabbing into the animals' flesh. One or two animals which gained the bank were cut down by natives who raced for the shore in anticipation of a few making it that far. Then, as quickly as it started, the action subsided, and a whole herd would have been wiped out.

On one occasion we hauled aboard two wounded piglets, and to my amazement one of them had had one foreleg ripped out of its socket and a back leg crudely severed at the knee. I asked how that had happened.

'A big fish,' was the answer. It seemed virtually impossible that any fish or crocodile could have joined in the melee and I continued to marvel at how this fate befell it.

When not pig-sticking I tried to find out why Frank felt that he was helping the local people.

K.I.N.G.M.I. stands for the Gospel Tabernacle Christian Church of Indonesia, and it was started and promoted by the Christian and Missionary Alliance, an American organisation. Some of the first missionaries to the Kayan in the 1930s had no doubts as to what they objected to in native life; the following quotations are taken from letters written by a missionary at the time: 'This dance is something that will be cast off very quickly once the light of the Gospel penetrates the Dyak (refering to Kenyahs and Kayans) heart . . . the rhythm and grace of these dances is undeniable, and yet they too will vanish with other heathen customs when the Lord Jesus comes into their lives.'

At Long Daha in 1941, 'It took three days for Potu and several other missionaries to collect charms, fetishes, ritual paraphernalia and human skulls from the five longhouses and destroy them by burning or dumping them in the river.'

I expect the natives regretted their action when the Japanese entered shortly afterwards and gave them hell.

However good the intention of the church may be, it seems to be mainly responsible for the mass migration from tribal lands, and the elimination of a way of life.

All ceremonies and festivities that had grown up over centuries to cater for the needs of these people are being wiped out. The arduous journeys to the coast to collect salt and sugar were an adventure and a test of manhood for the boys. No longer do they have to make these trips, so instead of going away on a six month trip to the coast the young men just leave altogether.

Under the constant criticisms of native pastors the people lose pride in themselves and in their way of life, and in the wake of this interference what does one usually find now? Just a gypsy encampment, yearly drained by migrants, filled by depressed remnants dressed in the rags that they have been prevailed upon to wear, spending their evenings dozing in front of a pastor spelling out the path to salvation.

This is the lot of most Christian longhouses, and what did Frank Peters think of it after training native pastors for three years?

'I've never actually been upriver.'

'Do you speak any of the native dialects?'

'No.'

'Do you know the customs and ideas behind Bungan?'

'What is Bungan?'

'Bungan is the system that you are replacing out here.'

'What do you believe in?'

'In leaving people alone.'

This sort of conversation was not conducive to getting co-operation for a flight out, but I had seen so much of the confusion created by missionaries that I had itched for a chance to have a discussion with them.

On another occasion, after reading one of their books on evangelising West Irian where they had met stiff resistance from the locals, I asked Frank, 'How do you justify imposing yourselves on people when they clearly demonstrate that they don't want you?'

He looked pained at the question and answered after some thought. 'Because we believe.'

It sounded like any political extremist explaining and justifying his actions. I tried again.

'When you see Muslims and members of other religions demonstrating equal certainty in their beliefs, don't you feel certain doubts?'

He had an answer for this. 'Ah, but Christianity has proved itself. Jesus Christ was the only prophet to say that he would rise from the dead and did.'

Whatever Frank and his colleague were teaching his pupil pastors at Long Bia, the practical side of their Christianity fell well below the natural Christian principles and actions demonstrated at pagan longhouses. The people may suspect this themselves but many also realise their need to learn to grapple with Western civilisation, and the missionaries are their only source of information. The natives themselves realise that the world is changing and that unless they can change themselves they are in danger of being wiped out. To this end they themselves request the missionaries to come to teach them and change their way of life.

It was impossible to get any help in finding a boat that was going downriver. The natives first replied that they did not know and, secondly that as there were six white people running the place I should seek assistance from them, but of course Marvin the pilot had already demonstrated his lack of willingness to help. He suggested I go to the strip every time he took off in case somebody dropped out.

I spent four days running two miles back and forth with my baggage only to find that if somebody did drop out another person was waiting to take his place.

I then moved to a hut nearer the strip to wait and wait. The hut was overcrowded with natives; most went out during the day, but one, who was an imbecile, remained stuffing pillows with fluff from a plant. At night-time the place crawled with rats and continually throughout the night I would wake to feel one nibbling my hair.

During the day a madman would start his antics outside a nearby hut. His favourite ploy was to put on ridiculous walks. He was very fat and this helped to make his contorted perambulations even more bizarre. Whenever children passed he pretended to be a chicken and squawked loudly. In between times he would find some object and examine it by nodding his head lower and lower; as the object and his head were about to make contact he stopped the nodding and tilted his face so that one eye was half an inch from the object and then let out a terrific squawk. This continued all day.

Each evening I went to see Marvin to ask about his schedule for the following day. It was always the same story of a full booking. One evening I explained that my visa and jungle pass had expired and could I now be considered a priority case?

He leaned back in his comfortable chair and explained how God was behind everything. We should not worry or try to escape from His all-powerful influence.

That evening I met an American missionary who had just been transferred to Kalimantan from assisting in a Vietnamese leprosarium. She explained to me that her first duty was to spread the word of God and to convert. If giving help to people by providing medicine and transport promoted the evangelical cause

A Kenyah version of blind man's bluff, in a Baram longhouse.

then they would do it; apart from that they were not interested.

'It is beautiful to see the radiant expression on a newly converted leper's face. How marvellous it is if we can get to these people before they die.'

She seemed to welcome the defenceless position of the lepers and the easier task in converting them.

I asked her, 'What do you think happened to the leprosariums when the North Vietnamese took over?'

Somehow I was not surprised when she simply replied, 'We used to say the best thing the Vietcong could do with these people was to line them all up and shoot them.'

On the tenth day of my sojourn I visited the local policeman and put my case to him. He acted at once, unpacked a uniform, squeezed into a pair of jungle boots, pomaded his hair, strode up to Marv's bungalow and ordered him, God or no God, to take me to Tarakan.

This was obviously a relief to Marv's wife who immediately took the chance to come to Tarakan herself for a few days. Marv was friendly to the end. I expect he considered that God was behind the actions of the local policeman.

In a broad context it may be a good thing that native people, who used to have their lives complicated by all sorts of superstitions, should be weaned away from these to a more stable system. Naturally in the halfway process they may feel the need rigidly to follow a new set of rules; but as Bungan was a recent pagan rule book that released the natives from many of the tiresome old taboos it can be seen that they were in fact evolving their own system and had no need of outside interference.

Marv flew us over the tortuous channels cutting through the swamps like miles of silver string on green cloth, and out over the stretch of sea dividing Tarakan from the mainland.

I landed at Tarakan just five months after setting out, but it had not seemed that long, for all the way tantalising routes, amazing objects and fascinating people had presented themselves. Being unfettered by plans or programmes I had been able to dally where I wanted and change course at a moment's notice. The enticing evenings lolling on the verandah, with the hills, the river, the palms swaying against the sky and the patter of the girls' feet on the boards as they danced to a background of tinkling sapes and flickering oil lamps, their tuneful chanting and the borak working round the blood vessels will always remain ingrained as the most memorable and attractive aspects of my journeying in the interior of Kalimantan. It is dying fast and I hope to be able to return before it is only a memory, or a minor anthropological detail in the annals of Borneo.

I had been intending to hand my jungle permit back to the police at Tanjung Selor, but as I had now by-passed this place, I decided to give it to the police in Tarakan. I felt like reciprocating all the help I had received from the Indonesian officials.

I sat in the police waiting room, with maps decorating the walls, while my pass, with chops from notables such as the headman at Long Metun, was taken to be inspected in a back room.

'Can I go?'

'No, you must wait here.'

I waited and waited.

Finally a lean officer speaking perfect English appeared and without formalities said, 'We would like to know what you have been doing in the border areas and our intelligence section is going to ask a few questions. Please follow me, it is in another building.'

I gulped; images of having my feet tickled while I tried to explain what I had been doing flashed through my mind. 'Just a second, I'm sure it's not necessary. I've explained everything to the police at Tanjung Selor and I would have given them the pass only I came straight from Long Bia.'

He looked at me wonderingly.

I risked further explanations. 'I only brought this pass back in here to help you with your records, keep them straight, you know.'

He pondered on this, could not see where it was wrong, and sent me on my way.

Next stop was the immigration officer to get my visa brought up to date so that I could leave the country.

With these problems ironed out it should have been easy to go, but I had forgotten the previous trouble I had with Indonesian airlines.

I booked a scheduled flight on a Norman Islander bound for Tawau, in Sabah, Malaysia. After arriving at the airport I was duly informed that unless another passenger came they would cancel the flight. Half an hour after the plane was due to leave, a Chinese Filipino turned up at the airport, and whether he intended going to Tawau or not he ended up providing the excuse for the pilot to take off and away we went.

At Tawau airport there were the inevitable delays, and I decided to give way to a craving that had been building up from eight hours' walking a day and a low calory diet. I ate a steady stream of chocolate bars and ice cream, much to the horror of a group of Chinese girls representing a school hockey team on their way to Labuan. I had trimmed off thirty-five pounds and could afford such luxuries.

Weeks later in another town a powerful looking girl came up to me and said, 'Weren't you the person eating chocolate and ice cream at Tawau airport? Where did you get such an appetite?'

'From going for a stroll through Borneo.'

14

Pupil of the Penans

Back in London, with a comfortably expanding waistline, I soon developed an overwhelming desire to return to see what was 'over the next hill'. Besides, I had not, and still have not, completed my intended purpose of travelling across Borneo from west to east in one continuous trip. However, leaving that in the back of my mind, I intended to make several excursions in the central highlands of Borneo, which seem to me to combine the most attractive features of the island.

Another important plan was to spend time staying with the Penan people to try to learn more about their way of life and absorb some of the tranquillity of their personalities.

Bario was to be the base for my various plans, and I had arranged with one of the longhouse headmen on a previous trip for a room in which I could store my equipment and come and go as I pleased. My addition to the longhouse reversed, in its small way, the trend of the young people leaving for the coast in search of jobs, so I was made especially welcome.

Before the Bario airstrip was built in the 1960s (for military use during Indonesia's confrontation with Malaysia) there were two main routes down to Lio Matoh on the Baram, where it was possible to pick up boats heading for the coast and points in between. The more popular of these routes is via Long Banga, tracking the Apoh Duat range that divides Sarawak from Kalimantan. The other, via Long Lellang, is more hilly and is used mostly by Penans. My plan, therefore, was to stay with Penans in the Pa'Tik area near Bario for about a couple of weeks and then make my way south to Lio Matoh via Long Lellang, down the Baram river a little way, and then up the Silat river to join up with some more Penans there. Thence I hoped to make my way across the top of the Linau river again, possibly seeing some of my Penan Apoh friends or maybe the Penan Busang whom I failed to reach with Tujok on his trading expedition up the Linau river. From the Apoh region I would cross the border dividing range to Ikeng Luri to revisit the Penan Kihan group in Kalimantan with whom I had stayed the previous year.

Finally I planned to retrace my steps of the previous year to Long Kelawit, where the longhouses had been attractively laid out around a central green, and then as far as Long Nawang, whence I could at last make that long planned border crossing (albeit reversed) into Sarawak to Long Busang and so on down to Long Jawi.

It was a long trip where much of it would involve making our own paths from the lie of the contours. I was excited both by the physical challenge and the chance to revisit old acquaintances. With my previous experience I hoped I could quickly get on with the purpose of my trip and circumvent much of the tiresome bureaucracy into which I had blundered as a novice.

I left London in the middle of March, 1979, with light snow falling, and with the enticing prospect of emerging at the other end into pleasant tropical warmth. As usual the plane was delayed a little while but when the engines were finally given full throttle and we swished forward two wheel pins broke and we came to a grinding halt. The woman next to me fainted, and then unfortunately revived because I quickly had to hold the paper vomit bag in front of her while she transferred the contents of her last meal into it. As I performed this gruesome task I felt that nothing ahead was going to be so unpleasant and tried to put the experience down to some preliminary toughening-up.

The flight was eventful in another way. After Damascus, pungent aroma floated back from the seat in front. It turned out to be a dental nurse smoking marijuana and trying to disguise the smell by continually spraying the air with cheap scent. A few words with her revealed that she had finished a five-year stint in London and was returning, complete with a Cockney accent, to work in Brunei. When we parted company in Brunei we wished one another bon voyage in our chosen occupations, both no doubt reflecting on the unlikely travelling companions that one passes on the road.

I quickly made my way to Miri in Sarawak and called on the friendly immigration official, who snapped a three-month chop into my passport in a manner that suggested a conspiratorial understanding of my spiritual need to have a lengthy sojourn in the jungle. As usual I delayed in Marudi waiting for a flight to Bario but used the time profitably by spending evenings with the Southwells

Hudson and Winsome Southwell in Marudi.

listening to reminiscences of their sixty years in Borneo. Also in Marudi was a VSO teacher called Chris Bell, who ensured I woke up in the morning by assembling the whole school outside the government resthouse where I was staying and having them sing a rousing song. As soon as I had blearily acknowledged them from one of the fort-like windows they would be dismissed back to their classrooms.

After several days I got a seat up to Bario, and without further ado joined a gentleman called Padera Ulun who was just setting off to stay with some Penans in the Pa'Tik area. When we reached the Penan encampment I explained that I was a complete jungle novice and merely wanted to learn what I could and share their way of life for a short while if they thought they could put up with me. They considered the matter carefully but I could see they were secretly happy and flattered, and I was assigned old Ala Bujang as my Penan tutor. For the next three weeks he endeavoured to turn me into a competent jungle dweller. We built sulaps, mixed up poison, went hunting, collected rotan and generally lived the life of jungle nomads.

The Penans generally stay for a month or two at the top of a hill and once the hunting becomes reduced move to a nearby hilltop. There are, however, other groups who live at a lower level all the time. Living at such a high location obviously meant only a small amount of water could be used for cooking, and any washing had to be done when one happened to be at a lower level where there was a stream. Consequently there was a distinctive smell most of the time, mostly reminiscent of drying meat, but because of their scanty clothing not the particularly virulent variety of body odour that might otherwise have been the case.

Tidiness was everything in such cramped shelters, and my clobber compared unfavourably with Ala Bujang who possessed two brass earrings (worn), one loincloth (worn), one sarong, one shirt, one blowpipe, one bamboo carrying container for darts, poison and associated equipment, one gourd container for dart 'flights', one parang, one rotan basket, two strips of sewn-together palm leaves for (a) applying to part of the roof shelter, (b) wrapping up sarong and shirt, and (c) putting on top of logs for sleeping on with the end section left unrolled to serve as a pillow.

The Penans around Pa'Tik are a loose knit community and there was much coming or going from Batu Lawi where the hunting was good and where they clearly felt more in charge of their own territory and less imposed upon by the Kelabits or other visitors (such as myself).

After hunting, preparing sago was the most important task and it was unisexual work. The men cut down two or three palms close to the base of the trunk and trim off the fronds where they branch away from the trunk, being careful to remove any edible shoots first. This leaves a log about six feet long which they roll down the hill to a suitable washing site. At the bottom of the hill the trunks are split in half and the pith gouged out with a sharp stick used like an adze. Meanwhile the women are setting up an apparatus on the edge of the stream which basically consists of two mats suspended one above the other by the use of a wooden frame. Then the sago pith is placed on the top mat, water is added and, as with grapes, the mixture is stamped and squeezed with the feet. The sediment flows through holes in the top mat to the bottom mat, which has a finer weave.

When the process is finished, the sediment is rolled up in the mat. It looks like putty and feels like sand, but it stays stuck together. It is then dried over a fire and crumbled into a brown flour which can be stored for a considerable time if necessary. Three six-foot trunks take about a morning to prepare and fill half a large biscuit tin, so it is possible to draw a comparison between that and the work of preparing rice.

One of the ways of preparing the flour for consumption results in a fairly glutinous compound, so special 'sago forks' are made with

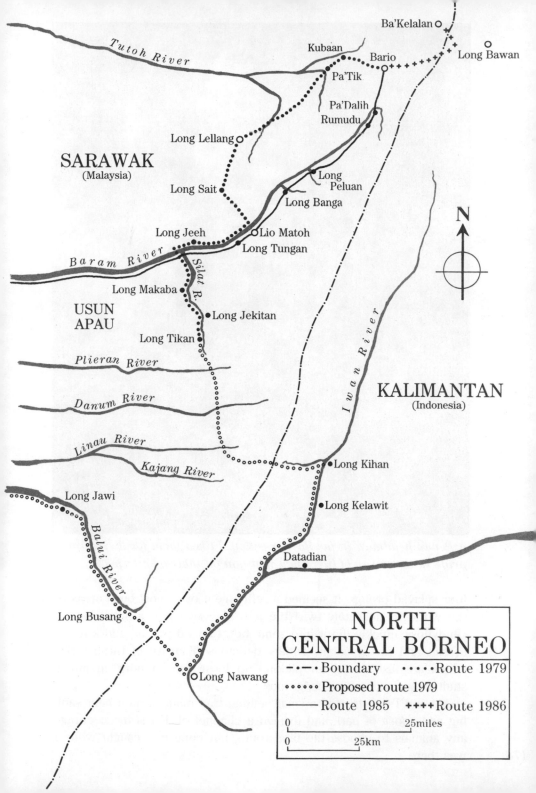

A Penan headman in the Baram valley. I liked them for their innate pride in their way of life. They met you on their own terms.

four splayed prongs. It seemed a refinement over most bush areas of the world to delicately twirl the jelly-like sago into a small ball of candyfloss, quickly dip it into some hot, thinned pig fat, add a touch of salt and finally eat it. Totally delicious. The use of these forks, which are also useful for picking up loose bits of pork, in jungle shelters seemed quite incongruous.

Ala and I constructed a small animal trap made from a bent sapling and noose of bark and formed a channel of debris to encourage any animals to choose the fatal route, but none was caught while I was there.

Mixing up the poison for the blowpipe darts and making the darts is another time-consuming and important occupation. A cut is made in the parir tree and a small container fixed below it for the milky sap to drip into. It is then dried to form a black, solid lump, and when required is reheated and the dart points dipped into it.

One day I was dissecting a block of the black poison for my own amateur interest to see if anything had been added to the sap while I was not watching. I was using my fingernails to crumble it into small fragments when Ala, who had impressed upon me never to touch it with bare hands, saw what I was doing and immediately insisted I wash my hands as thoroughly as possible in the nearest stream (some distance away), and not to touch any more, but his action came too late.

Some of the poison had been absorbed through the thin membrane beneath my fingernails, and I expect some had brushed against the many small cuts that one's hands permanently have in the jungle. Suddenly my heart started beating very rapidly, and I felt as if I were going to faint. I lay down, my mouth went dry and my limbs started shaking slightly and I could not lift them. After about an hour I recovered, but I had had first hand experience of being parir poisoned, and it is not to be recommended. In making darts for his blowpipes, Ala carefully cut a notch near the tip so that the poisoned end would break off in the animal on impact.

I enjoyed the constant flow between the different groups in the Pa'Tik area. Ala Bujang himself obviously liked the variety of joining a hunting party working a pig round a valley with a pack of dogs while the younger men performed the physically tiring and skilful work of rushing about with spears, and then moving on to another group where he would eat a few of their tasty morsels and relate the hunt he had just been involved in. In a way he was a sort of bard, a jack of all trades and this no doubt was why he was appointed to look after me. In almost everything he did ran a vein of humour. He would wake in the morning with an inevitable loud yawn and the words, '*Sujuk-bah* (cold)', and within a minute had rolled up his entire possessions and packed them into his carrying basket.

He would pick up one of the babies and start dandling it roughly about while making a noise like a kookaburra at it. The baby at first seemed to imagine it was being handled by a normal person, but soon the shaking and unearthly squawkings had it bawling and with a cackle Ala Bujang would pass it carefully back across the fire to its mother.

One day I showed him a photograph of a Penan group I had taken some time before. He studied it carefully and pointed at one of the women and said, 'If I had a wife like that I'd be the happiest Penan in the jungle.' Although Ala complained of the cold when he got up in the morning, I was surprised how many of the Penan slept with just a loincloth and without any warmth from a fire. They did not bother to stoke up the fire until they got up in the morning.

A further impression that lingers was the mournful notes of the nose flutes that the young women used to play in the early evenings while sending their babies off to sleep. Like the rest of the women, they worked long hours after dark by the light of burning dammar resin or a type of compacted insect excretia, making the handicrafts for which they are renowned and which they use for trade.

The noticeable feature of groups moving fluidly around the same general area, such a Pa'Tik, seemed to be that it was done with no apparent disagreement or bad feelings. Everything seemed to be arranged with good humour and I cannot recall ever hearing a raised voice. Obviously areas of jungle have to be left fallow for a time for game to restock itself and I imagine their system could be similar to the Anglo-saxon method of land usage in England before the Normans arrived with their concept of permanent land owner-ship chiefly, ironically, for the purpose of hunting.

The Penans from the youngest age are somehow aware of the role they fill within the whole concept of their own and the forest's con-tinuing prosperity. They know one and the other are interlinked and in general are unsuperstitious. The only time I saw them unsettled by anything natural was by a sudden deafening clap of thunder from a clear sky. At this they pulled out some of their children's hair and threw it to the ground as a sort of offering while incantating various things. As I could pick out the word 'Tuhan' or God several times, I wondered whether the Christian influence from Bario had not contributed to this dramatic reaction; and my own presence may have contributed as well.

During about three weeks I saw enough of their way of life to want to stay longer and learn more about their settled activities, but I was there first and foremost as a casual observer, tarrying at the expense of their natural hospitality before satisfying my other wish to share their essentially nomadic life and to 'see over the next hill'. Also, I needed to keep an eye on my visa date, and with a lot of ground to cover and many possibilities of things going wrong I decided, when a group of Penans were returning to the Long Lellang area following Easter celebrations in Bario, to accompany them. First however, they wanted to get clearance from the penghulu in Bario so that they would not be held responsible for any mishap that might befall me on the way.

15

Long Makaba

We duly trundled into the plain of Bah and up the little hill atop which stretches the complex of Ulung Palang, the headquarters of the penghulu. It was Easter time, so a variety of religious celebrations had been planned; indeed one was in progress when we arrived with two senior politicians dignifying the proceedings: Luhat Wan, the federal deputy minister of agriculture, and himself a Kayan from the Tutoh, and Balan Seling, the Sarawak minister of home affairs, who is married to the penghulu's daughter.

The Penans and I were politely ushered into the gathering, where it was assumed we had come from spiritual conviction. The hovering, helpful assistants issued us with pamphlets and guided the Penans to a darkened area near the back while I was placed between the two VIPs. Clearly etiquette demanded that we stay awhile, and I surrendered the notion that I would be grinding my way up the hills of the Halleluiah Highlands for another day. The Penans I knew would be happy to drink some cups of warm milk (the local beverage) and would not consider a day earlier or later of any consequence. Anyway, if they did . . . had they not wanted to come and have this little chat?

Prayers and singing followed one another with the words 'Tuhan' and 'Halleluiah' imprinting themselves indelibly on my mind. A preacher took a chapter from Galatians as his text and sternly warned the sober, hardworking audience to refrain from all sorts of temptations that seemed unlikely would ever come their way.

Eventually food was served and general conversation ensued. My two neighbours, on discovering what I had been doing, were keen to ask my impressions and opinions on local development and how to help the Penan community. Now religion and politics are taboo subjects in most countries, and I should have known better than to wade in with honest answers and helpful suggestions. The penghulu and one or two other local policymakers were listening to our conversation and before long different Kelabit factions were advising me, for different reasons, not to get involved.

Luhat Wan (who welcomed any new views) wanted to help the Penans by supplying them with basic aids such as hoes, parangs and seeds, while the penghulu wanted to go further and have a government programme to help them settle down. Harmony was restored to our discussions with a humorous story by Luhat Wan about his trip to President Carter's peanut farm in the United States. He did not, however, consider it prudent to extend his humour into a lighthearted suggestion of a Penan peanut farm, and neither did I.

The session ended with some more spirited Halleluiahs which seemed to revive the penghulu's spirits and he happily approved my trek through his domain. So, with a few hours of daylight left, the Penans and I hurried away up the first steep hill to make our way to an old sulap at the base of a hill near a stream before nightfall. My weeks of wandering over the rugged hills paid dividends during this forced march and I arrived in reasonably fit shape. The bogie of Friday the 13th (that was the day) was beaten, and I looked forward to the days of jungle bashing ahead.

There were fifteen Penans returning to Long Kerong from the Easter celebration, and the shelter was only about fourteen feet long. I took up about two feet six inches of it, so the others lay entwined like a basketful of dogs. Before curling up for the night we feasted on a pig that had been shot along the way.

The next day became a sort of leave-taking ceremony with various Penans from around the area drifting into our little jungle clearing to wish us well, pass on messages and nibble on the pork. Old Ala Bujang, my Penan guru and mentor during much of my stay in the jungle, was one of them. We laughed together over some of the incidents we had shared but soon he left saying, 'Don't forget me,' I have not. Nine years later his memory is still fresh and I have the feeling that I am bound to see him again sometime, perhaps on his normal beat around Batu Lawi.

Gradually the people in our party began to become distinguishable by their little characteristics. One man was virtually deaf and dumb, another hawked and spat unrelentingly with a distinctive three phase noise pattern. Sometimes the children would amuse themselves mimicking him in unison only keeping just one noise ahead. It was very funny. At one point of the day we gathered some sago palm shoots and nibbled on them sociably.

While waiting to leave Bario I had talked to Gloria Paya Ibun, a Penan girl from Pa'Beraan. She explained that the Penans interpreted Christianity differently from the Kelabits, but as far as the outward manifestations were concerned my group seemed to have been inspired by their visit. Prayers were held before meals or hunting trips, before almost anything, even the prospect of climbing a steep and slippery hill.

I spent the rest of the day in the sulap reading a book I had picked up in Bario. There is much to be said for not carrying your own reading material, because making do with whatever is available can lead in unlikely and entertaining directions. The title of this shipwrecked paperback from Bario was 'The Toff and the Great Illusion', and was an escape back to city life. Occasionally I sampled one of the pork snackettes that had been laid out according to type : Fat, brazed crisp skin, tender and fatty skin, intestinal strips, vital organs, and a pot of soup made from the watery, bloody juice in which the pork was cooked thickened with a little sago flour.

In order to travel as light as possible I had left my blanket and all surplus kit in Bario and was hoping that a nylon anorak with a hood would keep out the highland chill, but as I lay on my back on the uneven poles I had to concentrate on trying to relax and not shiver. Fortunately, before the coldest part of the night at about five o'clock, everybody rose, and the fire was stoked up. But this was not the prelude to an early start. It was Sunday, and nobody felt they should move after the spiritual recharging they had gone through at the Easter celebrations in Bario. So throughout the day prayers and other religious manifestations were interrupted only by light meals of sago baked in pig fat, and sago mixed with pig fat, wrapped in leaves and then baked. Very tasty it was too.

After I had chanted as many Halleluiahs as I thought appropriate, I wandered off following the rocky steep course of the Kebaan river. Selecting a pleasant dappled rock which divided the narrow river, I lay down to while away an hour or two. Two Penans appeared walking along the bank, one of whom I recognised. I decided to give a Penan signal, and keeping quite still whistled briefly in the way that means "freeze". The effect was instantaneous. As one, they dropped to a crouch turning at the same time, and remained immobile as they surveyed the scene.

It did not take them long to spot me despite my being partially obscured. I enjoyed my little triumph as there are all sorts of whistles and jungle noises, and only the right note would have had the desired effect. We returned together, but my walking was not as polished as my whistling, and the Penan dogs jumped and shied at my noisy (though normal to me) manner of moving.

Back at the sulap, knots of Penans were huddled together chanting hymns and songs of praise out of tune. Two of them seemed to be instructing the others, and the same people who, before attending Easter at Bario had happily smoked, now felt obliged to forgo this little luxury.

On Monday morning we were finally away, and I set myself the task of trying to persuade the children to show me where they picked up the little edible titbits that they constantly foraged for along the path. In this way I was introduced to two new fern shoots, and more exciting . . . my first edible wild root! It is a common conception that jungle folk or stranded travellers feed off wild shoots and roots, but until now I had never seen any wild roots being eaten, and that, I have to admit, was only through prompting rather than choice. Tapioca root is of course eaten extensively but it is cultivated, and I have never seen it growing wild.

We were vaguely following the course of the Kebaan river in the direction of Pa'Tik. It meant going up and down steep and slippery hills to avoid a long meandering course, and along flatish paths that were covered in loose stones and rocky rubble that was scarcely easier going than the hills. We soon passed a place that for me was familiar, where an elderly and ill Penan was staying. He had been built a high platform where he sat crouched all day. His hands and feet were swollen and he shook spasmodically. Different people took it in turns to stay there and look after him. His daughter and son-in-law were there then, and I had seen two others performing these duties on previous visits. It was a sad human scene that is played out all over the world but the lonely isolation gave it added poignancy. It must be miserable to become redundant and inactive in a lifestyle that centres on physical activity. I imagine that the weight of depression has a corresponding physical effect which expedites the course of the disease.

Our progress was slow because of an old lady with a swollen neck, but I was glad to be on the move and the steady pace gave me opportunities to investigate little things along the way. We stopped at Pa'Kebaan for the night where there many kinds of fruit trees, including a lemon that I would guess was planted during confrontation (there was still a lot of army debris around). Unfortunately only a type of pear was ripe. The children gorged themselves on it while at the same time nibbling on large grass shoots; did one prevent indigestion from the other?

That evening we sat down to an extensive vegetarian meal of rice, ferns, leaves, mushrooms and sago. I had brought the rice with me from Bario but the Penans regard it in the same way that the Kelabits regard bread : very pleasant as a 'vegetable' but not suitable as 'food'. After eating rice they would fill up on sago.

At Pa'Kebaan there was a young woman heavily pregnant, resting in anticipation of the appointed hour. I found myself reflecting that in such a sparsely populated area, where birth and death become so significant, her alpha seemed like God's answer to the omega of the poor man on his perch back along the track.

The next day the group spread out, with me and the less active people heading straight for Pa'Tik while the others made hunting detours. On the track a group of monkeys seemed to be outraged by us and descended screeching. They followed closely making threatening noises for several hundred yards.

When everybody had finally gathered at the beautiful site of Pa'Tik we had a choice of pig, barking deer and bat wing, which I found myself nibbling on more for the experience than the sustenance. In one of the huts we found an old tin of pig fat that was full of flies and cockroaches. Undeterred, one of the religious instructors boiled this mixture while constantly dipping in a rotan scoop to which the foreign bodies stuck while the fat dripped back into the container. When the fat was mostly clear, various delicacies such as animal eyes and brains were fried in it to produce some exotic jungle canapes.

More prayers in the evening. I was beginning to get into the routine and concluded that it is easier to be religiously minded in an agrarian community where the hard day's labour, lack of entertainment and thankfulness that the crops are growing massage the higher senses.

The next morning as dawn awakened the ripples on the Kebaan river I became aware that the instructor, who had eaten a good helping of the pig fat, was being violently sick. Whether his sickness was physically or psychologically contagious I do not know but before long several of the group seemed to be very unwell. In a momentary relapse from his seediness the instructor told me that he did not usually go into jungle, as though I might understand his plight. Perplexed and agitated, I went down to the shallow, wide river to plunge into the cool water and jolt myself into considering what all this might mean.

I returned to find that a swift conference had decided that three members of the group (a man, a woman and me) still unaffected by the mystery illness should hurry on to Long Lellang. With appropriate adieus the three of us moved off from the wide clearing on its grassy knoll with the beautiful views of river and mountains, back into the twilight and alluring world of primary jungle.

The woman may have been fitter than the others but she still had appalling catarrh, and I was interested to see her periodically digging up a little root, crushing it and inhaling the vapours. My theory for their ill health was their contact with unfamiliar germs in the 'Big Smoke' of Bario, so it was ironic that their reason for going there — to receive religious instruction — was being put to immediate use in praying fervently for recovery from the repercussions of that visit.

We followed a small river up its rocky and slippery course. It was geologically interesting but killing on soft feet. The studs on my football boots slipped hopelessly on the wet mossy rocks. Like wet and dry weather tyres, studs are good on soft muddy ground and bad on rocks and logs while "trainers" are excellent on logs and rocks but a failure on steep muddy hills. However, on balance, football boots are best.

The man collected some sago palm hearts along the way. A monkey that boldly presented itself, screeching noisily, had its belly pincushioned with blowpipe darts, but it moved away and we lost it before it died. Many hornbills whirred overhead, and one or two sitters were lucky not to be hit by the blowgunner. The average blowpiper gets about two pigs a week while somebody equipped with a gun can get as much game as he likes. In that situation a single man can support quite a large group.

We arrived at Sungai Tabah, and the remains of an old sulap, in the afternoon, and set about organising a meal which consisted of mushrooms collected along the way, cooked in water and pig fat, and sago shoots, again collected en route, chipped and boiled with sago flour. There were also some rice that I had brought, some dry kijang meat made palatable with some salt, and finally some sticky condensed milk boiled with a little coffee. It was an impressive spread.

The sores on my feet had started to fester again, and I decided to experiment by not treating them at all and seeing if they would build up a local resistence.

For some reason the woman started to make a new sulap, using bark strips for roof covering, despite the man offering to sleep on the firewood shelf of the one already prepared. In the event, we all slept under the new shelter. Periodically during the night, as in the day, the woman coughed up a rumbling stream of phlegm, but at the same time this prompted her to stoke up the fire, so we all kept nice and warm.

The route from Sungai Tabah was the usual up and down. On the low level paths there was the constant hazard of thorns tearing at one's skin and clothing. One particularly annoying tentacle is a mass of tiny, slanted barbs can be extracted only the way they went in. We passed a dammar tree and the man collected a lump of its resin, which is used for lighting because it burns slowly like a candle.

Towards the latter part of the day it became a frustrating walk although there were not so many hills. It had been raining and the nasty, stripey highland leeches were out in swarms, and they made raw patches around my ankles. Unlike the friendly, black ones, the stripey ones attach themselves painfully.

We were constantly traversing around hills, which is a strain on the ankles, and following no path, with hidden roots competing with the vines that caught on the framework of my pack. We stopped at the top of a hill where there were the remains of a sulap. Nearby was a tiny, still, shallow patch of water about two yards square; even laying my water bottle sideways I could only quarter fill it.

All day I had looked forward to bathing my stinging legs in a cool stream and washing off the mud gathered from walking across the pig rootling areas, but clearly we were stopping here for a reason (perhaps good hunting). Additionally there was the unusual feature of a plague of flies.

It was all so uncomfortable I had to do something to take my mind off things and volunteered to make the fire. The man meanwhile went off hunting with his blowpipe while the woman collected shoots from the palm whose leaves, when young and unfolded, are used for stitching together to make pouches, or when more mature are roughly woven together with split slivers of the stem to form a waterproof roof covering.

Once I had the fire going I boiled up a milk and coffee cocktail as a crumb of comfort against my stinging, aching body. The man returned with a kijang and we ate the tender tasty bits (the veins in its neck filled with a white mush were memorably good.) During the night they smoked much of the remaining meat.

After a more or less tolerably comfortable night where I was thankful it did not rain, I woke early and in the few moments before shaking my limbs into life surveyed the distinctive scene: the morning sun creeping through the overhead canopy, the fire being blown up, the mist clearing from among the trees and the good earthy smell. With the prospect of reaching Long Lellang at midday, the walk was more relaxed, but I was still conscious of the drag I caused to the man whose progress past logs, gullies, rocks and thorns was so speedy he had continually to wait for me. The woman seemed in better health, and busied herself with a variety of small activities depending on whether she was walking or resting: either gathering edible titbits, pointing out things of interest to me, such as edible leaves and fruits, or splitting rotan for the weaving of mats and baskets.

Presently there were signs that a kampong was not far away, and by early afternoon we arrived at Long Lellang, positioned at the top of the Akar river. Only very few people were at this beautiful long-house and only for the purpose of collecting the many fruits that had ripened at the same time: nanka belanda, durians, oranges, pomalo, rambutan, pineapple and other obscurer ones; but my current favorite — buah abong — had finished three or four weeks earlier.

After this refreshing stop we carried on to where the Penans had an encampment. Indeed they told me they had been around here for nine years. Their semi-settled lifestyle seemed unsatisfactory without the inclination or technical knowledge of a settled existence, and clearly this is the debate that the government is trying to solve.

The predominant feeling would seem to be represented by the Kelabit penghulu, who sees their settling down as the only course of 'progress' and any other suggestion as in the 'touristical interests' of people who want to preserve a primitive lifestyle.

Later, in the new kampong of Long Lellang, where the government was building an airstrip, I heard that the area had been designated a Penan area where a proper settlement programme would be tried. This would certainly make more sense than encouraging nomadic people to lose their traditional skills without teaching them new ones.

Intriguing though other people's problems were, however, I had my own to worry about. Adding to the mass of sores collected along the way, I had picked up a heavy cold which had moved to my chest and stayed there. At the settlement I took my leave of the helpful, obliging Penan man and woman, resisted the offer of a 'powerful' blowpipe that could send a dart 'through a pig', and returned to the old longhouse at Long Lellang to spend the night. I passed the old airstrip built during confrontation — its steepness must have made landing and taking off difficult — and saw that grazing buffalo still kept it in serviceable shape.

From Long Lellang I was again faced with finding my way, but the people in these parts are helpful and undemanding. I was told to follow the river, and doing this had a pleasant, sunny walk of an hour or so before reaching the new kampong. Few recreations are more enjoyable than a highland walk on a sunny day along a river bank dotted with shade trees.

188
The new kampong was a bit of a shock because it was merely a

rough collection of shacks. Apparently this was a temporary measure while an airstrip and a permanent longhouse were built. Furthermore, many of the Kelabits were moving to Bario, Marudi or Miri, impeding the progress of the building works.

I met a government settlement officer who was based at the Penan area at Long Sahip. He too felt that the settlement policy was inconclusive and more distracting than helpful. If he tried to enforce policy by sternness the children merely ran off into the jungle not to return. Their parents said they wanted the children with them to 'share their food'. The officer emphasised that the Penans' tradition of freedom reacted badly to the demands of settled life. It sounded like an attempt to persuade Gypsies to give up their caravans for houses; an impossible task.

He mentioned a further irritant in which missionaries urged the Penans to stop using their traditional medicinal cures. Poor Penans! Told by the government to settle but given little effective direction, urged by missionaries to give up their beliefs and medicines, no wonder they are reluctant to accept the interference of well-wishers.

In Long Lellang the religious revival that I had already experienced in Bario was particularly deep-rooted, and commands such as 'to love one's neighbour' were taken so literally that people were embracing when they met on a jungle path (not that it happened to me), and the sight of a crucifix produced shaking sobs. The service I attended here seemed straightforward enough with singing, swaying and handclapping, but the text was Galatians, as in Bario, and again everybody seemed to be accused of much more than they had probably been up to.

The headman returned in the evening after a week's fishing trip with a large collection of bamboo tubes filled with smoked fish flesh. The next day was Sunday and nobody was moving anywhere, so I was sped on my way with nothing more than 'God go with you', which in fact proved enough to get me to Long Sait after passing through another Penan community at Long Keban.

Long Sait is a mini-HQ complete with two teachers, and I stayed with one of them called Martin Ibu. He was more in tune with the government on local policy and had completed a charm-destroying ceremony that morning. The charms were very simple affairs made from animal hair, skin, bone, roots and leaves.

The next day we decided to go to the Penan settlement at Long Kerong, about an hour away, to do some fishing with nets. When we arrived an elderly woman was in a state of hysteria shouting and calling on Yesus Christus to do something. My sudden and unlikely appearance may have convinced her that some sort of extraterrestrial action had been taken because she quickly settled down and behaved normally. Some of my original Penan party came from Long Kerong, and people were anxious to know why they had not returned. I was able to reassure them that their ill colleagues were being treated in the approved manner (with all my listeners holding one another tightly and calling on God's divine mercy).

After lunch I decided to walk on alone to Ba'Pulau, which is on the way to Lio Matoh, where I was told there was a shelter. I made one false start, and had to return, and was then shown a completely different track. It always helps to be shown the correct track at least ten minutes outside a settlement because so many converge near a village.

On my second attempt I walked for about three hours before reaching an area of old cultivation densely overgrown and cut by a meandering river. All around were high hills. I had not the slightest idea where to go. The route was into the river and along it (to avoid the dense vegetation) and then at some point to get out — but where?

A little used track leading from a river can be invisible to the inexperienced eye . . . but I was no longer inexperienced. Summoning up all the bushcraft I had learned over the previous few weeks I branched off up a trackless hill, using topographical instinct only. Over the hill and using a meandering route to descend, I came across a light track and steamed off along it.

The worry, exertion and accumulation of sores produced an exhaustion that made the going very hard. My ankles had hardened septic patches, very painful to the slightest touch or knock. Similarly, my pack and wet clothes had rubbed my sore patches raw. However, I doggedly kept to the track, hoping it would lead to Ba'Palau and not to an extinct camp.

As darkness approached I was mentally set to spend the night at the next stream; but suddenly I came into a slightly open area, and there was a Penan. I whistled softly in the appropriate manner so as not to frighten him away by suddenly appearing. He spoke a little

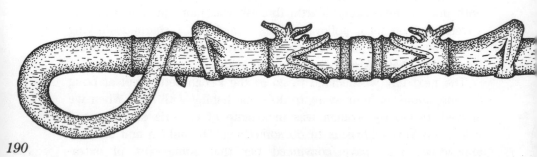

Malay and showed me to the empty shelter at Ba'Pulau. He too was staying there the night, and we boiled up an unripe papaya that I had picked up from the patch of abandoned cultivation.

Afterwards we communicated with our pidgin Malay and he explained how he had acted as guide to a European who walked from Lio Matoh to Limbang. He described the man as a very strong and fast walker and I suspect the journey had something to do with confrontation. Whatever the circumstances, it was impressive to hear of somebody having his walking ability endorsed by a Penan.

From Ba'Pulau it was only a few hours to Lio Matoh, and my friendly Penan put me on the right track so that all my energy could be concentrated on the physical aspects of the walk. I arrived in Lio Matoh relieved at the prospect of getting some medications (western ones) for my legs, and with the pleasant sensation of having arrived. I was especially grateful to two government health workers, named Rowland and Moses, who happened to be there and helped me in many ways. As a bonus they both possessed a good sense of humour that made all dealings with them a pleasure.

I travelled with them to Long Tungan, the next longhouse down from Lio Matoh, where they were to install a water system. Their work involved heating pipes in order to bend them to the correct angle for fitting. Getting the right heat while bending the pipe in the correct place proved an almost impossible task. Rowland cursed and shouted advice as Moses struggled and sweated. A curious band of natives watched the proceedings as though they were some sort of entertainment and not part of a project that was for their benefit, and that perhaps a little assistance might have been appropriate.

In the evening it was announced there would be 'Bugis dancing', an expression new to me, but its origin soon became obvious. Participants jerked about wildly in stiff limbed contortions as if they had been ordered to go demented in a prescribed area, while a tinny ghetto blaster with tired batteries pulsated whatever the fashionable noise was at the time. Clearly 'Bugis dancing' had been in-

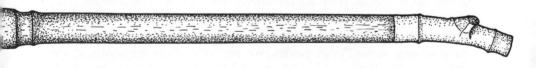

A wood carving from a Baram longhouse.

vented from Moses' struggles with his pipes during the afternoon. Judging from its popularity, I would not be surprised if it has not survived until today, and could add a lively dimension to the best efforts of western jivers.

I was trying to give the sores of my feet a chance to heal with the medicine supplied at Lio Matoh, but the constant wet and sweat rendered the medicine useless and the pain remained excruciating.

From Long Tungah we (I had now become part of the health team) moved downstream to Long Semiyang, a seventeen-door Kenyah longhouse, where we were swiftly filled up with booze and ordered to 'play' by some very playful girls. The leader, called Corrie Bungan, soon had the boys playing local musical instruments like sapes while the girls enthusiastically performed local dances. It was all spontaneous, enjoyable and probably how things used to happen in the past.

My main consideration at this point was whether to go over to Indonesia via Long Moh, as was now being suggested to me, or up the Silat river as planned. Different locals favoured both routes, and in the end after another all-night party at Long Selaan, where the headman's wife had described the locally distilled arak as poison, I decided to go to Long Makaba on the Silat, close to a Penan community at Long Jekitan.

First, however, there was a wedding ceremony at Long Selaan to be got over with, which involved two days of complicated unbridled festivities. Rowland and Moses were in the thick of it in constant entanglements both between themselves and with the longhouse community.

There was a great deal of shuttling by canoe, some of it motorised, between nearby longhouses and the longer the festivities continued the more dangerous the excursions became. I counted myself lucky when I finally got down to Long Jeeh unscathed. It was a B.E.M. longhouse, and in contrast to the Catholic longhouses further up-river no drinking was allowed, which under the circumstances was something of a relief.

The headman's son, who also acted as the local headmaster, was going up the Silat river to do some trading with the Penans. He offered to take me to Long Makaba, where we could get details of the approximate route over to the Iwan river in Kalimantan, and hope-fully arrange some Penan guides. We set off early in the morning up the beautiful Silat river, which constantly changes levels according to the rainfall and thus presents a correspondingly changing set of hazards to negotiate.

Few people go up the Silat river as it is off the main Baram river, so any visitors are especially welcome. We arrived at Long Makaba and stayed there for a couple of hours to discuss the route, and then proceeded on to the Penan settlement at Long Jekitan, where I was assured I could get a couple of men to come with me.

A fairly uncomfortable night due to the large number of people staying in the shelter was compensated for by there indeed being two men apparently happy to act as guides. We moved on upstream to Long Tikan, where the following sections lay ahead:

Two days walk

Plieran River

Make boat and go upriver one day or walk two days

Long Sagau

Two days' hill walking

Danum River

Walk five days (cross border here?)

Long Adan

Make boat. One day

Ikeng Luri

Walk one day

Iwan River

Walk one day

Kelawit River etc., to Long Nawang, Long Busang, Long Jawi and back down the Balui River.

It looked fairly daunting and my two Penan companions, knowing that I wanted to go to Long Busang most of all, favoured going by a much more direct and easier route. They wanted to go to Long Luar on the Plieran river across to Long Geng, and on to the Balui and upriver to Long Busang.

I lay in the hut and wondered what to do. In spite of my fatigue from several weeks' physical effort and a week of poisoning from home-distilled arak, I should have pushed on. But when I woke in the morning I made a fateful decision to return to Long Makaba to regather my strength and to see again a girl who had distracted my attention by the simple ploy of using my thigh as a workbench on which to roll a cheroot while I was trying to concentrate on the route being planned to Kalimantan.

One man I know makes it a rule never to change plans because of the suggestions or actions of a girl. In retrospect it is a rule I should have followed too, but that is another story. The rest of my trip was postponed. I excused myself by maintaining that by preserving my health I would live to battle another day. In other words a tactical retreat, and if recuperating meant being in the company of a charming Kenyah girl and her family, then so much the better.

16

Bario twice revisited

A further visit to Borneo resulted when a sporting friend took stock of my flabby physical condition and bet me that I could not run the 1986 London Marathon in under three hours fortyfive minutes. The opportunity stirred me out of my citified torpor. If I could get fit enough to run fortytwo kilometres, I would win enough to re-enter that alluring world under what has been called 'the enchanted canopy'. More, I would be able to enjoy myself as much at the beginning of my excursion as at the end, when I normally get properly fit.

I knew where I wanted to go. Hudson Southwell, one of the founders of the B.E.M., had encouraged me during a meeting in Australia to visit Ba'Kelalan in the Kelabit highlands, where a guru named Agung Bangau was conjuring up miracles. Lights appeared in the sky, bottles of cooking oil refilled themselves and incurably sick people were getting better. I wanted to see it for myself.

To my sporting friend's surprise and chagrin, after many early morning runs and alcohol-free weeks I cruised over the marathon's finishing line in three hours and fortythree minutes. Suddenly I was reasonably fit, free and with some loose change jingling in my pocket. I lost no time in booking an airline ticket eastwards.

Things started well in Borneo. I got my pass with a minimum of trouble and the flight from Miri to Bario was the first I had made on a clear day. With the help of a map I could pick out every significant landmark, and the pilot also entered into the sightseeing spirit by flying within touching distance of Mount Mulu. New timber tracks snaked their way around the hill contours, and river tributaries glistened underneath overhanging branches.

The usual crowd of anxious passengers and loitering locals were grouped around the airstrip building. I am always relieved to step out of a plane, especially a small one, and Bario in the unhumid sunshine must be one of the nicest places to do it. My first impression however was that the World Within, as Tom Harrisson called it, had absorbed a little more of the World Without, for a chapter of motorcycle and scooter riders were idling and revving their infernal machines.

Coupled to this, an incessant buzzing of chain saws was echoing round the great plain like a stereophonic orchestra of mammoth cicadas. Clearly civilisation now lay a little further down the track, so without further ado I hurried away in the direction of Pa'Ukat, Indonesia and Ba'Kelalan.

Even as far as Pa'Ukat the occasional motor-cyclist whirred past me so I decided to go on to Pa'Lungan for the night. I was well cared for, and the only tiresome incident was the persistent badgering of a 'fifth form failure' (the new scourge of the interior for they are good for nothing) to hire a guide at twenty Malaysian dollars a day for three days. I happily and voluntarily pay ten or twenty dollars a night for accommodation, but resist unneccesary services.

In the morning I found that a man was going to Ba'Kelalan anyway to see his daughter, and obviously would prefer to be paid to do so as well. We set off at marathon pace and after a couple of hours he crumpled at the side of the path. I wondered whether he would appreciate my asking twenty dollars from him to carry his bags. As a guide he was superfluous as I remembered the track from going along it to Indonesia in 1978.

He stuffed himself with rice and dried pork which soon gave him some extra strength and we were off again. He complained constantly but we reached Pa'Rupai in Indonesia in the late morning, walked on to Long Medang and had a glass of water with a friendly family, and then followed the track back into Malaysia, down a narrow hillside gully and along a beautiful stretch of padi fields and drainage ditches to arrive at Ba'Kelalan at about three o'clock.

A former border scout took charge of me and we went along to see the headmaster, Rowland Satu. On the way he told of an incident where an American girl was deserted by her guide, got lost between Pa'Rupai and Pa'Lungan, and spent at least one night alone in the jungle. I was interested in this unprompted story because I knew the girl and was familiar with some details of the incident. It was good to get confirmation.

Rowland Satu's father had been taught by Southwell and was very willing to be of assistance. By a further happy coincidence, Rowland had made a study of Agung Bangau's miracles and written a paper on them. I urged him to make a copy and send it to Mr

Southwell which I heard later he had done.

A day's notice was needed to see Agung. No doubt he needed time to consider whether I was friend or foe, spy or disciple. Therefore the following morning I walked along the length of the valley, through a succession of villages such as Long Rusu, Budu Bui and Budu Aru before arriving at Pa'Tawing, where there is a small pastor's college, and where my travelling companion had come to see his daughter. A pleasant lunch was followed by a stroll back along the valley in the company of another 'fifth form failure' who had been helping lead buffalo from Long Bawan in Indonesia to Long Semado in Malaysia.

Back at Rowland's house I was interested to see a solar panel nestling on the roof. Apparently it was sufficient to charge up a battery that powered a light and his tape recorder after the generator had been switched off in the evening. Two or three visitors had just arrived at his house and were still exhilarated from their long cross-country walk. They stowed their carrying baskets and sat down to exchange all the usual pleasantries among passing strangers in the ulu.

Later that evening when we had finished our rice and pork, and would have been smoking a cheroot if it were allowed, Rowland indicated that the time had arrived to visit Agung. By the light of two small torches, their batteries hovering on the brink of extinction, we stumbled the few hundred yards to Agung's quarters, but we could not find a way in. The house appeared to be in complete darkness with all entrances locked. Just as I thought the trip had been in vain, the silent figure of his wife opened the back door and with a friendly gesture welcomed us in, and up to the first floor.

Around a large L-shaped room lit by a few oil lamps, a hushed throng, mostly women, sat with bowed heads while a man whom I took to be Agung sat to one side, his face obscured in a shadow, murmuring a low dirge. Occasionally a general response was called for, which was called enthusiastically. Agung stopped talking and was followed by individual women spontaneously praying aloud. This lasted another half hour and I began to wonder if it was the build-up to a manifestation or part of an all-night service.

Suddenly, however, it stopped. The participants as though released from a spell started chattering to one another about everyday topics. Agung emerged from his darkened spot and came to talk to us. My first impression was the striking facial resemblance and manner to the clairvoyant who lives below me in London. It had nothing to do with a penetrating gaze or mystical air. Both have a slightly pinched, sallow look, but a direct and friendly manner.

Agung made me feel welcome and I passed on messages from

Southwell. He explained how he wanted to broaden his audience and visit Australia and Britain. I pointed out that he faced problems speaking no English, but than I tried to remember whether Uri Geller, the fork bender, could speak English, and the fact that I could not proves it was not important. Soon, in the impatient, blunt Western way, I got to the heart of the business: What about these miracles, and was there a chance of witnessing one? 'Now you're asking something,' would be an accurate translation of his answer, but it took a lot longer to say than that. It seemed that he was working towards a date and a location yet to be decided. It was important that he should decide soon because hundreds of people would want to go there and prepare for it by making special costumes.

While he was talking I was trying to see if there was anything strange about the room. A little lamp attached to the wall seemed to be burning with a horizontal flame, like a gas jet. Was this just something I had not come across before or an extension of his miraculous fire shows? Alas, decorum did not allow closer inspection, and presently we said our adieus and retraced our tracks. It was not a totally successful visit.

In the morning I wished many thanks to Rowland Satu and stepped out for Bario. The journey back was uneventful but for a confrontation with a snake which had similarities with an incident several years before in Indonesia. The path was good and I was jogging lightly, paying more attention to the surrounding jungle than the ground in front of me, when I came within a millisecond of stepping on a snake coiled up on the path.

Hurriedly moving back, I hoped that my presence and noise would encourage it to move off. It did not and as it was in a place very difficult to go round I decided to lob a stick on to it. The effect was instantaneous. It swung upwards, its neck extended. The lower half of the snake was browny black, the top half dark green, and its extended neck was green with white markings.

I then got a larger stick and whacked it whereupon it moved away. My feelings of relief were soon replaced by inward admonishment about being too casual in a potentially dangerous environment. If I had stepped on it and had my leg bitten . . . no more marathons or anything else.

Back in Bario I decided to stay a couple of days and visit some old friends. I find this a rewarding experience because I think that people are genuinely touched if you take the trouble to seek them out again. One or two of the longhouses were even experiencing a slight population revival as a consequence of economic recession.

People fresh from being made redundant were rustily getting

back into the swing of rural life. The snazzy shirts straining against flabby bellies and winkle-picker loafers moulded around soft feet were being gingerly discarded in favour of more practical items. Perhaps they will even help to build new longhouses, but unfortunately the way things are I would guess that within a few years any new longhouses will be built specifically as tourist attractions.

Another visit to the highlands resulted when conditions fell into place for me to undertake the second part of my plan to walk from Bario to Lio Matoh, this time via Long Banga instead of Long Lellang. Topographically this was the easier route with paths of some description and the Baram river a constant reference point.

Our flight was the first into Bario for several days, and a noisy jostling mob was waiting to get out. Turnaround should take about twenty minutes but two hours after landing the overloading and overbooking still had not been sorted out. The situation seemed worse than I had ever known it and I was relieved that I intended to walk out.

The weather was sunny and the air fresh, and I met a man named Balla Tuan who intended going to Rumudu the next day. We trooped across the plain of Bah and up the rampart of Upper Ulang Palang. Although this was the penghulu's longhouse, I did not intend to waste his time with a courtesy visit and Balla Tuan just happened to be staying with some people nearby. It was shortly before Easter and preparations were under way for the type of festivities that I had experienced before.

In the process of renewing old aquaintances I called at the home of a senior citizen to ask about the baggage I had left behind on my last visit, when I had intended returning sooner rather than later. But he had left Bario for a month for the first time in his sixty years, locked up all his rooms, and taken the keys! This story has its point in that locks and keys were new. Greater wealth and greater mobility had made them neccessary. I cheered everybody up distributing some photographs I had taken on my previous visit.

Without my necessary equipment, I negotiated to buy a rotan carrying basket and one or two other useful items. While doing this I discovered that one of the women selling things had been with a family of Kelabits I had visited in 1978 when they were staying in a single farmhouse near an encampment of Penans at Pa'Beraan. The isolation had been too much for them and they had moved to Bario in 1983.

The next morning I was harnessed up and champing to get at the track when there was a delay while Balla Tuan decided that his wife would stay in Bario with their daughter, who was waiting for a flight out. Tears and hugs were followed by what seemed to be the same problem discussed in a hundred different ways, followed by more hugs and tears.

Finally we were away heading, not out towards Pa'Tik, but out past the airstrip. Although the plane was not expected, there were idlers hanging about who wanted to know all my details, which Balla Tuan patiently supplied. At last we were on the track to Pa'Main, Long Dano and Rumudu.

I had walked to Long Dano a couple of times before and although most of the path is a jungle motorway there are several turnoffs that need to be known, and in a relatively busy area new routes and paths are constantly being cut. We motored into Pa'Main at mid-day. This was the main Kelabit residential area before confrontation, but was considered too close to the Indonesian border for safety.

By two-thirty we had reached Long Dano where the assistant penghulu greeted us courteously, and presently we were on our way again. I noticed that the little airstrip had been completed since my last visit, and as we made our way to Rumudu a helicopter clattered overhead.

I had started the day fresh and with confidence, but by six o' clock when we reached Rumudu my legs had turned to rubber and the rotan shoulder straps were chafing my skin.

I had last come here in 1978 and this return visit was not a dis-sappointment. It is still a beautiful site on the loop of the upper Baram, with a well constructed longhouse. However, money filter-ing through from timber camps and oilfields had had many dif-ferent effects . . . good quality western clothes, improved cooking methods with a greater variety of vegetables grown, the kampong and interior of the longhouse very clean, flowers grown, cats treated like pets, no children with their ears cut, and nearly everybody else with their extended lobes snipped off. There was a piped water from the river supplying showers and lavatories, and there were chainsaws and outboards.

On the other hand, there was a new sense of insecurity with everything being locked up. With more consumer items and money around, the sudden acquisition of western goods is no longer con-spicuous. A white visitor no longer causes any interest and in a slightly disquieting development the children are not so polite and there are hints of the Indonesian 'Hello Mister'. The headman had lost some of his authority, with most of his people probably materi-ally richer than he was. One result of this was a failing code of hos-pitality and a lack of the noblesse oblige that all village chiefs had had.

Most of the 'useful' people had left for jobs in the cities and I was reminded of the same problem in many of the small South Sea islands that I visited recently. There was no doubt that the page had turned from the old to the new, and I count myself fortunate to have been there a few years before while the old spirit still existed.

I slept soundly despite aching limbs and in the morning had a sample of improved cuisine: sweet weak coffee, cracker biscuits, fresh fried barking-deer liver flavoured with garlic, finished off with a bowl of mata kuching fruit.

Much of the next day was spent trying to organise a guide to Long Peluan. Balla Tuan had originally volunteered but with his wife absent in Bario he had to do the chores and was forced to decline at the last moment. Instead I was helped by English-speaking Sandra, a mother of four children, whom I had known in Miri ten years before as a young gadabout. It was interesting that she preferred the ulu life of Rumudu to the tip-top life of Miri.

In the evening a friendly fellow came and chatted amiably, and I knew this was the run-up to a proposition. I had been softened up during the day and now came the offer . . . he thought he could just manage to take me, with the assistance of two friends, for two hundred Malaysian dollars. The offer was preposterous. Where was the willingness of the old? I quoted Sandra who had told me that they wanted to go to Long Peluan anyway to collect salt, 'Oh, we've already been while she was in Pa'Dalih,' he said.

I would not go higher than eighty-five dollars and the discussion ranged into the night. As we spoke a boar's head was silhouetted in the lamplight as it cooked on the fire, with a continuous foam-like eruption dribbling from its nostrils. At various times my hosts, a pleasant couple living next to Balla Tuan, changed the subject in order to keep a pleasant atmosphere.

Raya Balla and his wife were about fifty and of the old school. He had plucked out his eyebrows and had tattooed blue ones in their place, slightly arched, giving him an air of mild surprise.

Somewhat surprisingly we never managed to strike a deal during the evening's discussions, so it was left until the next day for somebody else to volunteer to guide me for the sum I had offered. Happier but ready for last-minute problems, I went off with Raya Balla to cut bamboo for fencing his padi-fields against marauding buffalo. The river was right up again because of rain in the night. This could be a problem as I had to cross the Baram about two hours from Rumudu. Alternativlely, my map showed a different route via Pa'Dalih and Batu Patong, but of course nobody knew it or wanted to try it — 'Only the old people know it'.

Well, I decided to go to Pa'Dalih anyway to see if anybody there knew the route. A brisk two hours along a good track brought me to the lovely kampong, but just as I arrived Sandra and the man who had volunteered to go with me were leaving (having collected one of her children). He was helping to carry some things for her. She told me that this man was 'useless' and 'can't even light a fire'. I looked at the little, bandy-legged, taciturn figure clutching a ghetto-blaster radio, and only vaguely registered her final words, 'His wife is as enormous as he is small and suffers from epilepsy.' He now wanted to go to Bario instead.

Nobody else was enthusiastic about leaving a comfortable long-house to go jungle bashing. Even on a straightforward mission of getting local information on typical weather patterns I drew a blank; two local teachers disagreed about which were the rainy months. At this point I decided to go on my own.

Sharp at six o'clock the next morning I got up and retraced my steps to Rumudu. There I decisively told the folks that I was off to Lio Matoh, and if anybody wanted to give assistance for double the normal rate but only half their rip-off rate they would be most welcome. A man stepped forward and for twenty dollars offered to help me across the Baram. Somebody else supplied three packets of cooked rice wrapped up in leaves, and without further ado, we were off.

Two hours of pleasant walking and we reached the Baram. There was an old boat on the far bank, and now my man earned his fee. He dived into the water, swam to the far bank, and brought the boat over. I pressed the limp notes into his hands, wished him goodbye, and rowed over to the other side.

Relief at getting started was now replaced by worry at finding my way. The gulf between finding one's way alone and with somebody else cannot be exaggerated; suddenly I had to provide all the answers. Additionally I was tired from the hassle and the extra walking to Pa'Dalih and back. I made a false start from the river bank by going over a hill and had to retrace my steps. After an hour of hard effort I had made precisely zero progress. Where was the jungle craft of six years ago? I felt very rusty and wondered at my confidence and impetuousness.

I then got on to what I thought was the right track and hurried along. Basically I had to make sure I did not go too far from the Baram, but jungle paths can be tortuous. I had also put myself under pressure by not taking enough food: three little packets of cooked rice for three days. However I pressed on, resting every hour to scrape off the many leeches. Then late in the afternoon, at the time when it usually began to rain, I reached 'Leppu Datu' — a hut near a durian tree that I had been told about. With considerable relief I stripped off, de-leeched, rinsed my clothes, stood under a waterfall, like a shower, in a nearby stream, and felt good.

In the hut I set up some strategic mosquito coils, sprayed a moat of insecticide around my sleeping area and lay down as dusk closed in on the battery of cicadas.

The rain in the night brought the leeches out in swarms in the morning. I set off feeling hungry, and soon became dog-tired constantly going up and down. Where the minor streams flowed towards the Baram I had to slither down, over, and then up again. At one place where a tree had fallen I could not find the path for at least half an hour. I sat down and ate one of the two remaining rice packets, which were rapidly going rotten, and reflected that it was April 1st — April Fool's Day.

Several times my legs just gave out, and I lay on the track seriously considering leaving my pack on the path and using my remaining energy to get to Long Peluan, but it did not come to that. In mid-afternoon I crossed the Okkan river, using a massive fallen trunk, and arrived at 'Leppu Wei' — 'rotan hut'. With great weariness I scraped off the leeches, sprayed the insecticide, threw my expensive 'guaranteed non-fail' (which had failed) torch exasperatedly into the bush, and tried to relax my aching limbs.

When I woke the next morning I ate what I could of the rotting rice, and prepared for a difficult day. Ruefully I thought that I was doing this for enjoyment. There were one big hill and a few mini ones but the going was generally quite good. I had no idea how far I had to go, and tried to conserve my energy as far as I could, resting and moving slowly and steadily on the hills.

By late morning I came to an area of old cultivation. With hope renewed I trundled on and reached the Beruang river, where I saw a Penan hut on the other side, and with a final effort waded the wide, fast-flowing river. When I was nearly across I saw that there was a rotan bridge further downstream . . . curses!

Inside the hut a family of Penans got over their surprise at finding a white man wandering alone in the jungle and gave me some bananas, tapioca root and boar broth. It could not have tasted better and had an instantaneous effect. I felt I could carry on, but the water from the river and the chafing clothes had produced the dreaded crotch rot. My rusty jungle craft had made me forget to take precaution against the debilitating condition, and I arrived at Long Peluan with only the thought of lying down.

It was another pleasant kampong (the people had moved from Batu Patong) with some building in progress although not many people around. The headman's quarters were clean and spacious with pictures of English footballers pinned to the walls. I lay on a split rotan mat, cocooned myself in a cloud of anti-mosquito smoke and contemplated alternately my stinging legs and a photograph of Pat Jennings at full stretch to a flying ball.

This kampong, though mostly Kelabit, marks the point where some Saban people live. They are a mixture of Kenyah and Kelabit, have their own dialect and live only here and at Long Banga, Long Puak and Long Tuah on the Bahau in Indonesia.

A long rest did me a power of good and in the misty, chilly, exhilarating dawn I ate some boiled wild boar, spinach and rice, washed down with hot sugarcane water. These items were thoughtfully provided by the headman, Tama Tuloyi Iwan, and he was doubly kind in putting me on the right track for Long Banga.

This section was a leisurely two hours' stroll. I crossed three rivers, two of them by rotan bridges, and followed a well trodden path. I was particularly pleased to arrive here because I had heard much about it from Hudson Southwell, and sure enough he was fondly remembered as 'Tuan Sapu' by the local people. This kampong also had its share of military activity during confrontation, and much debris is put to good use. It is a clean, inviting kampong with many individual homes bordered with flowers and fruit trees. If it were not so isolated everybody would want to have their weekend cottages there.

As is the way when sauntering along, a friendly person hailed me into his house and offered some fresh coconut water and slices of pomelo. He was Tama Anyie Jalan and he was about to set off for Long Puak, where his sister was Penghulu Tama Lasau's wife. As Long Puak was on my route and only about two hours further on, we went together and had an enjoyable chat.

At Long Puak, where the people had recently moved from Long Balong, there were a few Penans resting after carrying kerosene from Lio Matoh for the penghulu. They came from Long Lamai and I remembered that this was where so many Penans had died in 1978 from a virulent new strain of malaria. I was glad to hear that things had since settled down.

The penghulu's stepson, Anthony Lasau, spoke excellent English and told me many interesting stories about the area and people, including the time 'Tuan Maior' (Tom Harrisson) parachuted in and got tangled in the tree tops.

The following morning, after a breakfast that included particularly good varieties of mango and egg plant, it was explained that the people would not feel happy if anything happened to me on the remaining section to Lio Matoh and please would I give Tama Kassim fifty dollars for the privilege of escorting me? Now here was a fine example of human peversity: what would have happened if I had asked for a guide? Oooo, Aaaaa, very difficult lah, two hundred dollars, etc. I was under no illusion that Tama Kassim, whoever he might be, probably intended going to Lio Matoh anyway.

However, I was getting towards the end of my trip, and just beginning to get back into the swing of jungle craft and its etiquette, I decided to accept the proposed arrangement. Tama Kassim was then wheeled on. He was a little old man with a monkey skin hat, and slightly in the same mould as the proposed guide with the epileptic wife in Rumudu. In recommending him, Anthony Lasau had made an under-the-breath observation that he was 'very talkative', and this proved an understatement. In fact he spoke so much and asked so many questions (I now know how they must feel when I ask my questions) that he needed to rest every fifteen minutes or so.

I felt that I was responsible for him, and to add to this irritation, because we were going so slowly I let my concentration slip at one point and fell down a gully, landing heavily on my side. This provided Tama Kassim with the opportunity to chatter about how lucky it was that he was there to help me in this emergency. I felt like pulling his monkey skin hat over his face.

We carried on with him constantly saying, 'Slower, slower' and I decided the best thing was the course of least resistance, and dawdled about while he collected rotan or rested. Eventually we arrived on the Baram close to the river, where there was a solidly constructed hut with rows of personal effects of people who regularly passed that way.

Laboriously Tama Kassim began to organise his overnight stay while I worried that rain in the night would prevent us from crossing the Matapa river in the morning. In response to this Tama Kassim explained that Tuhan Allah would see us through and embarked on a mammoth praying session that allowed full rein to his verbal diarrhoea. Several times he said 'Amen', and as I started to move another torrent of words would pour forth. At the final 'Amen' I slumped forwards and began massaging the cramp out of my limbs.

It was a full moon and about midnight Tama Kassim got up and started cooking rice. Perhaps he thought it was dawn. Alternatively I hoped that he was not one of those people affected by the full moon. The prospect of Tama Kassim behaving strangely while wearing his monkey skin hat did not bear thinking about. Throughout the night it rained intermittently but dawn revealed the river at about the same height as the previous day.

With some relief I started my body engines with hot sugarcane juice, mushy rice and boiled pig from the dried pieces brought with us on rotan skewers, and finished off with a little papaya.

The Matapa river was quite easily negotiated and we then followed the outer bed of the Baram for a short distance before cutting inland for the inevitable up and down routine. The Tudan river presented a little problem; eventually we diverted to where a large tree trunk had fallen across the fastest flowing section; without it we could not have crossed. Then a high hill. Up and up we went. Rain started and Tama Kassim covered himself in a palmleaf hood so that he resembled a caterpillar. From the top of the hill there were impressive views of the Baram valley, and at one point of Lio Matoh itself.

In the early afternoon we descended a long, steep hill and stopped off at a natural swimming pool in a small river to spruce ourselves up for arrival in Lio Matoh.

However, when we got down to the Baram, there were no boats to get across. Instead there was a knot of Penans from Long Lamai

This Baram valley mother has already seen many changes — and the children in this picture will have to cope with many more.

sitting around, the woman dying rotan strips black and the men preparing to carry petrol and chainsaws to somewhere, probably the penghulu at Long Puak. Their casualness with the petrol made me think they were new to it, and no doubt following a few horrific accidents they will be more careful. It was another example of the encroachment of the modern world.

One of the Penans kindly swam the river in exchange for heavy payment of coin. At one point, he did not look as though he would make it, and I wondered how I would then stand with the others. A local headmaster once told me that two Penan boys he had employed to help him up some rapids had drowned, and the reaction from the others had been fatalistic rather than aggressive.

The Penan rowed a boat back, which we then took back over. It was still raining as we clambered up the long, notched log to a grassy clearing where three tin-roofed buildings, one similar to the government rest house in Marudi, sexagonal and fortlike, with two flags hanging limp from its poles, stood a little apologetically as symbols of the government's fiefdom.

There, in the misty, clammy atmosphere, a Saban, a Penan and a European respecfully knocked on the solid belian door to rouse a sleepy Upriver Agent who did not seem very interested in credentials or anything else, but did kindly offer a place to stay which meant sharing a washing area with a tethered river turtle.

Tama Kassim doffed his monkey skin hat, bid adieu in a long speech and went off to see a chum in the longhouse, and no doubt relate a long saga of the trip. In the meantime I imagine the citizens of Long Puak had been celebrating a welcome break from Kassim, and probably were congratulating themselves on engineering the whole thing. The Penan shimmered back into the mist, retiring and respectful to the end despite his all-important role.

The son-in-law of the Upriver Agent happened to be the headmaster of the school at Long Sait, and was in Lio Matoh at the time. He had been appointed to Long Sait at the end of 1979, after I had passed through in April, 1979, so we had a lot to talk about. Most notably, the Penan children are now encouraged by their parents to attend the school so that greater progress towards settling them is being made. He also mentioned that the completion of the airstrip at Long Lellang had meant an increase in visitors of all descriptions.

Once again Lio Matoh turned out to be the start of an enjoyable visit to the upper Baram and the renewing of some old acquaintances. Along the way from Bario, however, I made a mental note never to do this sort of exhausting excursion again, and if I was ever tempted to return to stick to leisurely canoe rides between longhouses.

At least, that was how I felt at the time. Now, back in London, I find myself looking at my maps once more and dreaming of a complete traverse of Borneo from west to east. Part of my route would lie through the Usun Apau plateau which lies between the Kelabit highlands and the coastal plains.

During one of my visits to Sarawak I was able to visit the plateau by a helicopter ferrying workers and materials to the site of a proposed 'millionaires club' — the joining fee would be one million Malaysian dollars. The idea was that it would be a cool and luxurious resort for weary politicians and tired businessmen.

In a little ceremony I signed the guest book as the club's first and (in the light of the events) possibly last visitor. Recession and an onset of commonsense later halted the absurd scheme, and it has since been abandoned to the tentacles of the jungle.

When I eventually visit the plateau again — weeks it will take without helicopters — I expect to find the clubhouse and holiday chalets in ruins, with snakes curled up on the beds and bars and argus pheasants strutting around on what was to have been a golf course.

This would be evidence of Borneo reasserting itself, and I would be sure to find more such indicators at other points along my route. Much is changing — but as someone once said, or should have said, the more Borneo changes the more it stays the same.